Don't Take It Personally

A Parent's Guide to Surviving Adolescence

John A. Davis, LCSW

Break Inn Books

Don't Take It Personally
A Parent's Guide to Surviving Adolescence

Published by:
Break Inn Books
1634 Walnut Street, Suite 111B
Boulder, Colorado 80302
Tel: (303) 440-7373 Fax: (303) 986-1416
www.breakinn.com

First Edition Paperback
Library of Congress Card Number: 2004092620
International Standard Book Number: 0-9754607-0-6

Printed in the United States of America

Cover Design by BK Media Group
Cover Photography by Molly McIntyre
Text Design by Marsi Buckmelter
Text set in Palatino

To Jeffy,
the most remarkable of parenting partners

and

To Zoë,
wondrous teenager that you are

Acknowledgements

I am so lucky. More than ever before, I am aware and appreciative of the people who make my life a growing and learning experience. However, these acknowledgements are about my book, so if you are one of the many, I'll say thanks to you in person.

There are a group of people who have helped me remove the manuscript for this book from the seat where I was sitting on it and make it live. Without their emotional support there is a great possibility I would still be using these pages for a pillow. Rick, Lisa, Christopher and Carolyn — you have helped me realize my dream. You have encouraged me, challenged me, listened to me talk about the same things over and over again, and almost never made me feel that you were getting tired of me. In all seriousness, your belief in the book (and me) drove me forward with a better belief in myself. I couldn't have reached here without your love and support.

I have to thank my sister, Susan, for pushing me lovingly to meet my success. And to my mom, Lois, for always believing in me.

In the nuts and bolts department, I have had great help. I want to thank Cody Oreck and Morgan Stanfield for editing my book so consciously and thoroughly. Bruce Oreck and Dave Rogers, you pointed me in the right direction to the right people at the right time. Marsi Buckmelter, Bradley Moss and Molly McIntyre, you took my written words and created a beautiful product.

There is another group of people who made this book possible and, in the process, gave me a sense of my self and my work that is priceless. Thank you to Patty, Kimmy, Steve, Jill and Mark, Donald, Christopher, Lois, Carolyn, Bernie, Karin, Susie, Stanley and Margo, Susie and Arnie, Mike, Norman and Charlotte, Rick, Lisa, Deborah, Katherine and Andy, Holli and Marcia, Barbara and Allen, Bruce, Karen and Kim, Ann and Flame and Scott.

Finally, to every one of my clients — I am so honored to share in your life's joys and sorrows. The work that we do together has taught me much, and it has helped me to help others.

Table of Contents

A Parent's Foreword

by Carolyn French

My daughter Ruby was on the cusp of that scary developmental time called Middle School when my husband and I divorced. While her dad and I had always parented well together, we were now parenting from separate houses and different lives. I was terrified that we'd blow it, that somehow we'd screw up and leave Ruby scarred for life. I wanted so much for her to be "okay" through this time. I feared she'd react to our divorce in unsafe ways. I was scared that she'd lose her way, and as a result we'd lose her.

I was in uncharted territory in my own new life, as well as in the blossoming adolescence of my daughter. I started to look in earnest for that ever-evasive, mythical Parenting Instructional Manual. I held tightly to the daughter I had known in elementary school. I sought advice from friends and other parents. But what I truly wanted (desperately) was an assurance that everything would be just fine.

Then my friend, John Davis, gave me a transcript of his book, a dedication penned on the first page: "To Carolyn: best wishes. I hope you don't screw Ruby up too badly. Love, John." I tried to laugh, but I was too scared.

This is quintessential John Davis: to acknowledge and honor with humor one's humanity, while lovingly directing us to greater understanding.

I have worn out the pages of this book. I've referred to it so many times that I can almost see the words I'm seeking before the page falls open. The beautiful thing is that John's wisdom consistently and lovingly requires that I remember my own. What do I believe? How am I holding the soul of this wonder who is my child? Am I focused on her wholeness or the circumstances of her hormone-infested world?

What I know is that my relationship with my daughter is richer as a result of reading this book. Now when Ruby and I disconnect and conflict, I'm better equipped to experience it in the context of who she is right now in her 14-year-old life. I understand a bit better the complexity, unpredictability and astounding resourcefulness of the young woman who shares my life, and my bathroom.

I get to have Ruby for another few years, and then she'll be off, out into the world. I look at the time ahead with a mixture of relish and unease. What sweetness and discord will these years unfold? How will our mother-daughter relationship weather them? Will we still be talking to each other on the other side? I'm already mourning Ruby's inevitable departure — and already planning my solo adventures to warm foreign countries.

Adolescence is a time of paradoxes for all of us, to be sure. I know of no other person who holds the weight and wonder of this time so lightly, so completely. John's words provide me with the courage to know that everything will indeed, be just fine. It may not look the way I thought it would, but if I trust in myself and my daughter, and stay true to what I believe, compassion and understanding will lead us through.

Enjoy.

Thomas Paine was probably a teenager
when he shouted, "Give me liberty, or give me death!"
I'm sure he was just yelling at his parents,
not the whole of England.

Chapter 1
The Big Picture

Survival Training

Our culture does a poor job of supporting teenagers. Generally speaking, we're afraid of teenage children. We look at teenagers not as human beings, but as human beings with problems and bad acne. Parents of these "creatures" spend too much time afraid of things that might destroy their teenagers. Of course, our culture's inability to embrace and educate teenagers is only half the problem. The rest of the craziness comes from teenagers themselves who haven't found a passion in life or even a direction in which to start looking for one. For someone "coming of age," with these components, it's understandable that Mommy and Daddy might become the target for all that is wrong in the world. It's not that simple, but let's start there.

A fragile relational space exists between a teenager's anger, insecurity and excitement for the future, their parents' sense of loss, and the balancing act that is the terror and hope parents hold for their children. This is the place where most families find themselves. It's a place that is rarely comfortable. Both parents and teenage children make each other the enemy in this familial purgatory. Friction among family members becomes the norm. It becomes easy to lose perspective. For the parent, the teenager becomes the identified problem. For the child, Mom and Dad are the issue. Frustrations grow. It is, as I often say to my clients working on substance abuse issues, enough to drive you to drink.

Mark Twain once said, "When I was a boy of 14, my father was so ignorant I could hardly stand to have the old man around. But when I got to be 21, I was astonished at how much the old man had learned in seven years!" Mr. Twain was correct — life with your child does get better...for all involved. Our children do grow out of their adolescence. I know several hundred twenty-somethings who are much more mature than their seventeen-year-old incarnations. I know a great number of teenagers who've learned to use their voices in a way that does not do damage to themselves or others. I also know parents who've learned to relax and trust their children in a manner that works for everyone.

Because you found this book, you probably know that there are numerous others available that can thoroughly help you understand the societal and peer pressures that our kids face. They trace adolescents' struggles to "back in the day." Most are academic. They are serious, informational and somewhat depressing, if you ask me.

Then, there is another set of books that prescribe a specific parenting technique to save your child. All you have to do is precisely follow the author's formula. They make good common sense. They're clear and concise. They also require you to parent just like someone who you've never met and from whom you may be fundamentally different. If you have a slightly different value system, oh well. As long as you change everything about yourself to fit the author's style, you'll be fine and your child will grow up to be an exemplary adult.

Believe me, there's no single way to survive your child's adolescence. You want some good advice for parenting your teen?

Stop looking for a single guru. Take what you like from every source available and leave the rest. Successfully parenting your teenager is not magic. It is not impossible. Staying sane and raising a healthy teenager is all about maintaining hope for your child and the future. You simply remember how much you love your child, and you work toward not being afraid of and for them. You maintain a fabulous sense of humor for about six years. Successfully raising a teenager requires that you learn to take care of yourself better than you ever have before. It requires that you know what all your limits are, and then demonstrate those limits to your child. Successfully parenting a teen requires creativity every day. You need to be conscious of your actions and choices as often as you are able.

Once Again, With Feeling

Let's get this straight — the experience you're having with your teenager is not unique. Though you're certainly contributing in all sorts of ways to your family's sanity, the negative events of adolescence are not created because of your bad parenting, or even because your child is possessed. Your teenager's actions are nothing personal. Your friends are struggling with their teenage children. Parents on farms, in small towns and suburbs, and those in major urban areas are dancing with their thirteen- to nineteen-year-olds over most of the same issues. Families are struggling with adolescents in similar ways in New Zealand and France.

Maybe the violence is worse here or alcohol consumption higher there. Big deal, the music is louder in your house. The language is a bit coarser in mine. The overall emotional, mental, spiritual, cognitive and relational issues are, as the Talking Heads chant, "same as it ever was." Throughout time and across cultures, teenagers have been screaming for acceptance and pushing against their families and communities in order to define themselves. They have to, in order to come to terms with the energy, confusion, spirit and hormones coursing through every fiber of their being.

Let me say that again with different language. *Teenagers have always acted out*. I'm guessing that Thomas Paine was a teenager when he shouted, "Give me liberty, or give me death!" I'm sure he was just yelling at his parents, not the whole of England. A number of years ago, my mother worked with psychotic adolescents at an in-patient hospital. I made the comment then that the term "psychotic adolescent" seems redundant. This observation was not meant as a put down to teenagers as much as recognition of the struggles of that time of life.

Adolescence is a time of immense confusion and strong feelings for everyone in the family. Think of it. As a teenager, your family always seems to be in your face. Your friends are everything to you. And your developmental work is the definition of yourself, by yourself. Few teenagers have the skills to accomplish this developmental task easily, or have the support to learn how. As a parent, your job is not to stop your children from acting like teenagers. In fact, it can't be done. Your job, your responsibility, is to love your teenager no matter what. Your work is to help your adolescent develop the skills necessary to survive herself and this developmental period of her life.

Please Read All Directions Before Proceeding

After working with teens for close to twenty years (and now having one of my own), I still like them a lot. We get along great. What you are about to read is most of the thoughts and suggestions for parents I've discovered over that time. Within the covers of this book you will find some very substantial strategies that you can try out on your very own guinea pig ... I mean, teen. These ideas will certainly assist you in taking care of yourself while raising a teenager.

Here is my very first suggestion. While you read this book (and long afterward) don't merely adopt my belief system. Focus your search for help on *your* parenting beliefs. Let your values, your life and your family be the guide through my ideas. Use my knowledge and experience to support your choices. If you only try on my beliefs, I might easily become another expert who didn't know what I was talking about, and who couldn't help with your crazy sixteen-year-old son. If you have no concept of what you believe, your starting place is this book. Don't forget — this book may be a gospel, but it's only the gospel of a nice Jewish boy living in the Wild West.

Don't take your adolescent or me personally. You should create your belief system from a relaxed parenting stance. It's your work to come up with, improvise and manufacture the strategies that work for you. As you can figure out what you believe about parenting, stay clear in this knowledge, and parent from your heart with love, you will survive your child's adolescence. In fact, you'll do more than just survive. There is a distinct possibility you'll feel pretty good about the child you raised. Wouldn't that be nice? I wish you the best of luck. With your kid, you're probably going to need it.

A teenager's world may change so often, parents often feel as if they don't know their child anymore.

Chapter 2

Do I Know You?

Too Much Water for the Banks

It starts with their feet. It's true. Our children start acting like teenagers the moment their bodies start to change, grow and mutate, and the feet are generally the first indication. Size sevens become size nines the following month. The next thing you know, hair starts gathering in places where it wasn't before. Your fledgling human being starts experiencing all sorts of new sensations. Bodily functions, generally experienced only by people of voting age, unceremoniously appear in your middle-schooler. Teens get taller, wider, oilier, smellier. Your child, literally, begins to grow out of herself.

The physical changes that are occurring within your child's body are rapid. Bones, muscle, tendons and tissue are constantly changing form. For some kids it can literally hurt to grow up. At the same time, the hormones in your child's body are surging like the Mighty

Mississippi after a torrential rain — too much water for the banks, if you know what I mean. It's volcanic inside your child's body, which probably explains zits. An adolescent experiences "the change" emotionally, mentally and cognitively. Your child does not feel or think in the same way. Hormonal change is also expressed behaviorally. Your son no longer acts in the same way. As often as not, his behavioral fluctuations will appear unpredictable and uncharacteristic. Remember the crack I made about psychotic adolescents? Physiologically, this is what I was talking about.

Your teen's sleep patterns will begin to shift. Getting plenty of sleep will now appeal to your teen. However, the 9:30 bedtime thing? Yeah, right mom. Your child's mind and body will have a harder time shutting off before eleven o'clock at night. Staying up until two or three in the morning does not strike me as abnormal. So in order to get the full complement of twelve hours of shut-eye, your log of a teenager will want to stay asleep until one in the afternoon. During the week, they have to get up at six or so to get to school. Do the math: twelve at night until six in the morning will never add up to enough sleep. Your daughter is not necessarily going to be very cheery forenoon.

Your son will eat more — or less. I know a certain five-foot, eleven-inch, fifteen-year-old who weighs about as much as a piece of rope, yet still manages to eat several hundred toaster waffles for breakfast. I can't quite figure out the metabolic rate it takes in order to burn the calories necessary to maintain that rail-thin frame, but there he is. Even sharks aren't that efficient, and they never stop moving. Or perhaps because of intense social pressures, your daughter will feel that a small salad and four gulps of air will be too much caloric intake. Neither extreme is pretty or healthy, but it's a possibility.

Your child's self image will shift. Acne can lock your daughter in her room for days at a time. Too much or too little chest, for either your son or daughter, can create intense agony. Clothes will become more and more important in expressing whatever the heck your teenager is trying to tell you. It doesn't matter whether it's Abercrombie & Fitch or an all-black ensemble with steel-toed boots. Looking the part, whatever part, takes a larger slice of the self-image pie for a few years.

It's a good possibility that smart-mouthing will become an unavoidable part of conversations with your teen. "Shut up" or "Leave me alone" might be among the nicest things you hear from your teenager. A number of my adult clients use the words "psychopath," "gutter mouth," "the evil one" and "tongue of fire" to describe the way their teenagers talk to them. Although you may seriously consider earplugs during your child's adolescent years, I wouldn't recommend them. Not hearing what your son is yelling at you is denial. It is much better for you to develop and maintain great boundaries for respect, as well as a sense of humor.

In so many ways, your child is, quite literally, no longer him or herself. Adolescents don't know who or what they are, and they don't know what they will become. It can be pretty frightening. So what does any self-respecting teen do when they become confused, frightened and directionless? Well, Adolescent Rule Number One states, "When you're not yourself, take it out on an adult."

What Adolescence Means To You

The experience for the caring, hip and groovy parent goes something like this: first, you appreciate your child for crossing the threshold into adolescence. You look at your child lovingly and tell your friends "What a remarkable manifestation of my child's physical maturation!" Two months later, you're calling the school, your parents and his friend's parents screaming, "WHAT THE HELL DID YOU DO TO MY CHILD!? I WAS NEVER LIKE THIS!!!" Suddenly and without warning, your child changes from a joyful, solid source of pride to something that resembles a grizzly bear being awakened from hibernation. Before I receive any hate mail from the grizzly bear lobby, I'd like to say that this statement isn't entirely fair. Grizzly bears may be ferocious and short-fused, but they don't get embarrassed or angered by their parents' every move.

When teenagers behave badly, there's no excuse, but there actually is a reason. Once upon a time, there lived this brilliant guy named Erik Erikson. When Erik was a teenager he went through a terrible identity crisis. Afterward, he joked that he had been so messed up that his life work was to figure out what had happened. Once Erikson had analyzed his own process, he developed a theory about what goes on for everyone. In fact, Dr. Erikson coined the term "identity crisis."

Erikson identified eight stages of psychosocial development that we all move through during our lives. He believed that if someone does not complete the developmental work of any one stage, he would have difficulty growing up and maturing. For example, in toddlerhood (which is just like adolescence, but with neater rooms) everyone's work is *Autonomy vs. Shame and Doubt*. That is, during this stage one learns to take control over certain portions of their life. For instance, if a child doesn't learn to use the toilet instead of his pants, he will develop shame about himself. It follows that he will begin to doubt his abilities to learn other skills or deal with his feelings.

During adolescence, Erikson labeled our developmental work *Identity vs. Role Confusion*. From years twelve to eighteen, our work is to develop a sense of identity through our occupation, sex role, politics, spirituality and relationships. This is what your kid is doing. Don't blame Erik Erikson for your kid's behavior. He hasn't come back from the grave to encourage your teenager to act the way she does. Erikson just recognized that all teens must work on *separation* from what they've known and accepted (what their families have told them to do) and move toward *individuation* (developing a belief system of their very own). One difficulty of figuring out what to do with your teenager is that she rarely responds in a linear or predictable fashion. Your teenage child (and everyone else's) will respond in diverse ways to your consistent parenting. She will find a way to rebel and express herself that is uniquely hers.

Just so you know, Dr. Erikson says that the developmental stage you, the parent, are in right now is *Generativity vs. Stagnation*. You're working in your life to find some way to satisfy and support the next generation (your bratty kid, for one). Your core work is to care for another. Parenting is supposed to be your focus. When you don't figure out how to support and encourage your young ones, you slow your own life's growth to a crawl. There is cruel irony here — your teenager wants nothing to do with you, but if you don't figure out how to be there for and with her (no matter how she manifests her adolescent separation and individuation) everyone in the family loses in the next phase of life.

Pushing Off

In traditional developmental theory, teenagers just do their separation and individuation, period. That sounds pretty nice sometimes. You wouldn't mind if your purple-haired son, fresh off of yelling at you for never understanding him nor respecting his privacy (you washed his clothes), left your house to live somewhere else for the next four years. It would certainly keep you from making reality of your running away fantasy — the one you've had ever since he told you he hated you three months ago, right after he asked for twenty dollars.

Unfortunately, our children actually follow less traditional developmental theories, which tell us that all separating and individuating happens in relationship to someone else: namely, you. In order for your child to mature beyond his current state, he must emotionally push off of someone to develop his own value and belief system. This process is inevitable.

Why Your Teen Acts the Way He Does

- *Your teen is having an identity crisis.*
- *He's defining himself outside of the family for the first time in his life. This is confusing!*
- *He doesn't have much life experience (no matter what he says), so he's trying out all sorts of new ways of thinking and being.*
- *His insecurity, combined with his desire to self-define, won't allow him to admit that anything is wrong.*
- *Your teen is making the transition from self-centered child to other-centered adult, but he's not there yet.*

I think of it this way: when we want to understand something, we must seek its opposite. For example, one must understand short to make sense of tall. You want to know wide? Find thin. Then, add the relative experience of the person looking for meaning in order to create real understanding. Take basketball skill, for example. Put me in a game with sixth graders and I dominate. To eleven-year-olds, I'm the next incarnation of Air Jordan. But put me in a game with NBA players and they run and soar by me like I was lying down. Any opposite only has true value within the context of personal experience. We live in a world of gray, not black and white. Nothing is as simple in life as one or the other.

With your son, life as it was (his preadolescence), is all that he knows. Something in the genetic make-up of our species insists that, as soon as his body starts to percolate with puberty, he come to know some other experience. No matter what your family experience is, your son will search for meaning elsewhere in the universe. He tries opposites first. This would be fine if the opposite was all he tried. You could adjust one hundred and eighty degrees in your parenting stratagem if it only happened once or twice. This is too simple. It takes more than just opposites for anyone, even your fourteen-year-old, to see the light at the end of his journey.

So your son tries a lot of things, in a lot of different ways. No matter where you parent, he moves somewhere else. He's bobbing and weaving away from your attempts at direction and control more gracefully than Muhammad Ali. Do not attempt to thwart his process. Not only will you be unsuccessful, you'll drive yourself batty. You'll also create a twenty-four-year-old that acts like a sixteen-year-old. He just won't live in your house with you anymore (or worse, he will).

The Dependence vs. Independence Conundrum

The way the *Dependence vs. Independence* developmental work takes form in the mind and soul of a teenager is rather interesting. First of all, thousands of times daily, your child is asking herself, "Who am I?" Not a bad question for any of us to ask ourselves. For a teenager however, this question does two things. To start, it pushes her farther from where she was before the question was asked. Remember: your daughter is moving away from what she knew to be true. This question constantly reminds her that she can no longer be Mommy's sweetheart.

At the age of thirteen or fifteen or eighteen, she doesn't have enough experience outside of sweetheartdom to know who she *is* going to become. Because you've raised your child at least somewhat appropriately, she does have some sort of valid value system. So she looks to those values (what you taught her) for answers. Which takes her back to her need to push away from what was. Which makes her ask herself, "Who am I?" And the whole struggle starts anew — with a little more intensity. Sooner or later, the grizzly bear awakens.

What occurs next is actually logical. The "Who am I?" confusion leads teens to try on all sorts of different styles. Different is key here. When I was a delightful preteen, my mother used to buy my dress clothes at Brooks Brothers. "Classic styling," she told me. During my childhood I never once complained about my blue blazer and gray slacks. In my teens though, there was no way I could wear that imperialistic, unimaginative, gross look without losing my identity. I started picking out my own dress clothes. I tried a number of different looks over the years that followed, and the ones I chose were even goofier than the classics. But that was the seventies, and another story. The point here is that I found it necessary to locate my own style by trying out several other looks. It was normal. Whatever form your teenager's experimentation takes, it too is probably normal.

Try Lots and Quit Fast Parenting

I was once given brilliant advice that I now regularly pass on to parents of teenagers. "Try lots and quit fast." In other words, don't waste your time with anything that fails you. Be creative and persistent in finding what works. Teenagers do this without being aware of what they are doing. They try on a value, a style or a behavior, and they wear it until it no longer feels comfortable. Then they try on the next fad. This happens on the average of 3.7 times each week for the average almost-adult. In fact, FAD means **F**or **A** **D**ay. For your daughter, grunge becomes goth becomes straight-edge. It may take a month or three years, but she will move all over the stylistic continuum. A teenager may change so often, that a parent might feel they don't know their child anymore.

This worries parents. Teens feel that worry and take it as a put down. Because teenagers don't really know who they are, they're insecure. They would never admit this to your face, of course, but it's true. So, anything spoken about your son, even in the most innocuous manner, makes him uneasy. Any put-down, perceived or real, creates too much self-doubt. Instead of owning this feeling, he pushes farther away from you. As a good parent, you worry more. And so it goes.

In addition, teenagers live in a world that is mostly black and white. Though she is gaining greater capacity for abstract learning, your almost-adult daughter is, for the most part, capable only of concrete thought when it comes to her own life. One day, black is correct, the next day, white. In your daughter's existence, no matter what hue shows, her way is the right way. When it comes to her parents, it rarely matters what you say. To your child, you'll either be wrong or she won't hear a word. The only two things that matter to your teen are (1) she believes what she believes and (2) friends are really important.

Friends, Friends

In no other stage of human development, will friends take on such mythic proportions. Lack of friends, a multitude of friends, the best friend, the girlfriend or boyfriend — they're everything to a teenager. For a teen, peers are number one, two and three in importance. Other people whom your kids know are a distant fourth. Friends also take up places five through eighteen. Parents and family come in 19th. It's not that family is a bad thing, even if your child acts like it is. The movement toward friends and away from Mom and Dad is a matter of developmental and psychic survival. To your teen, family is just confusion. Friends are, well, friendly confusion.

An interesting developmental tug-of-war occurs with friends. It's what I call the *Me-We Conundrum*. On one side of the rope, your daughter wants and needs to be fiercely independent from her family and all authority. Across the mud pit, which is parenting, she's dependent and needy with her peer group. Pull either way and everyone gets muddy. She still has to pull. At home, she demands to be however she wants to be. Then she leaves and acts like everyone else in her crew.

WHAT DO I BELIEVE?
Part 1

I want my child's friends to talk with me:

a. *Once, when I first meet them.*
b. *At least briefly, whenever I see them.*
c. *As often as is possible. Can I take you three to dinner?*
d. *Rarely, I never liked that kid anyway.*

My teenager can be with friends:

a. *Whenever he wants.*
b. *On the weekends whenever, during the week by agreement with me.*
c. *After homework, but before dinner.*
d. *Who says you're in charge?*

I want to meet the parents of my teen's friends:

a. *Now, give me their number please.*
b. *If and when it is convenient.*
c. *Only if your friend looks like trouble.*
d. *Never, I never did like that family.*

I have a friend whose seventeen-year-old son is a remarkable dancer. He dances at a studio that encourages parents to hang out, watch, and be part of the community. The son forbids his mother to stay. "She makes me feel too uncomfortable! I can't dance when she's here." He almost removes her from the studio bodily. So she leaves and, at times, feels frustrated. My friend rarely, if ever, gets to see her son move so beautifully and joyfully. She doesn't get to see him as a dancer or as a teacher to the youngest hip-hoppers he instructs in the studio.

As a parent, you rarely see the full picture. You see what your child not-so-graciously allows you to see. You don't see how she uses her life experience out in the world. Wouldn't it be nice if you could get a little perspective? Try this exercise to remind yourself that your daughter is developmentally and appropriately full of it. It might make you smile and help keep you sane. Next time you get into a spat with your daughter, don't take it personally. Let her tell you that you don't know what it is like to be 14. Let her rant on about her sense of personal style. You don't have to send her off with a hug and a kiss, but do send her off.

Then go to the mall. Watch a group of two or ten friends walking together or simply hanging out. They'll all be dressed identically. The shoelaces on their $95 Adidas will be unlaced in exactly the same fashion. Their Gap jeans will sag at exactly the same distance from their respective crotches. Their baseball cap bills will curve with precisely the same arc, and be adjusted on their heads in precisely the same way.

Take away the obscenely expensive clothing and the situation persists. Almost all groups of teenage friends will look alike, with minor variations. Now here is the key to the exercise: Imagine every one of those kids yelling some form of "You don't understand me!" and "I want to do it MY way!" to every one of their parents. Then remember, you are not alone. This is not your fault. It is what every teenager must do.

And More Friends

You may have had this conversation with your teenage daughter.

"Mom, I'm going out with some friends. I'll be home later."

"Who are you going to be with, honey?"

"I can't believe you still don't trust me. I mean, it's been three months since I stole the car! Just some friends, okay."

"I do trust you, dear. I wasn't thinking about the car... until now. I just want to know who you're with."

"Fine. I'll be with Serena and Terry. Satisfied!? Be home at 6. Bye."

"Alri ... Hello?"

All parents worry about their children's friends and their families. We want our not-so-little darlings to have "good friends" who are "good influences" and come from "good families." There is no denying this. Before my Zoë was born, I was a teacher and then a therapist. I'd never met a single kid I didn't like. In fact, even today, from a work standpoint, I like something about every teenager I meet. Yet when Zoë started having friends around our house, I discovered any number of kids who I couldn't stand. They didn't share well (of course, Zoë shared perfectly!). They weren't always honest (my daughter would never lie!). They were sometimes impolite (my angel had perfect manners!). I admit it — I was uncomfortable with Zoë playing with certain kids. I didn't like it when she was under the care of certain families.

While in elementary school, and during middle school to some extent, it's possible for a parent to have some say over friends. You can discourage your child from playing with certain kids, be unavailable to provide rides, or even tell little white lies to keep your child with the right friends. Of course, I've never done any of this, but as a professional, I've heard as much from other parents.

During adolescence, it becomes much harder for a parent to control peer influences. For all sorts of reasons, good, bad and indifferent, your kiddo is going to hook up with a few suspicious characters. You know that you can't, and shouldn't, try to control your teen's friendships. What the heck are you supposed to do? Develop a bleeding ulcer? I don't think so.

Start meeting your child's friends as early as you can. If you're reading this as your teen turns sixteen, start meeting his peers anyway.

When meeting your teenager's friends you should avoid certain faux pas at all costs. Don't sing old Beach Boys tunes on the first meeting ... no matter what. Don't wear shorts and black socks with sandals. Don't hug and kiss all over your child while the new friend is present. Don't worry though; you can be assured that almost anything else you say or do will still mortify your teen. As with everything else, treat his feelings with respect, but do what you have to do for you.

It *is* okay to ask questions of the friend if you don't cross-examine them. You can tell the difference between curious interest and interrogation easily. If a little voice in your head is saying, "This is just what my father did. I hated it when he did that. It makes sense to me now though," you're interrogating.

Once you know who the new friend is, invite him into your life once or twice. Ask him over for, or take him to, dinner. Take your embarrassed son and his unsuspecting friend to a movie. Talk some more. If something comes up that disturbs you, talk about it with the kids. I don't mean that you should talk with this friend as a parent, at least not completely. These other influences on your child aren't your responsibility, nor can you control them. So, talk to them as if they were worthy of your respect. Tell them your values. Tell them you really, truly do not want them to bring drugs and alcohol to your house (or whatever it is you want to say). Tell them you appreciate their respect. Then let them go about their lives. You won't get perfect compliance from your child's friends, but if you've laid out the ground rules beforehand, at least you're in a logical and reasonable place from which to have your knee-jerk reaction.

One more thing: talk to the parents of your kid's good friends. What the heck, talk to all of your teen's friends' families. Your adolescent is going to hate you for it. It shouldn't matter. One of the great losses our communities have suffered over the years is the disconnection of families and neighborhoods. I knew every one of my friends' parents. They knew who I was and had talked with my mother. If something happened, my mother heard about it. Having to deal with this parental-connection reality helped me avoid trouble on more than one occasion.

Ask your child's friends for their home numbers should you see them around more than once. Or get the numbers from your child. Call and say hello to the other parents, or e-mail them. Tell them that you have certain values that you would appreciate them supporting. Get a feel for who's on first. You don't have to be best friends with any of them, but the sharing of information will definitely lower the acid reflux in your stomach when your angel is out of your sight.

Faith and Teenagers

"Why is all this happening?" you ask. You've loved your son as much as you could. You've given your daughter everything she ever needed and quite a bit more that she just wanted. You've done your best to stay out of your not-so-little one's business. You just don't understand why you can't seem to avoid this remarkable pain and struggle.

Remember, "Who am I?" is the prevailing question. Teens don't yet know where they're going or exactly why. Junior *must* turn away from parental advice. He's insecure to the nth degree. For the most part, solitude, patience and trusting in the processes of life are something our culture didn't teach him before adolescence, so now he's scared. Friends deal with all this. They are the teenager's drug of choice. Friends are the opium of the teenage masses. Friends numb the pain. Friends know what friends are going through. They don't care if you are in trouble with your parents, the law or school. They don't care what you're wearing, as long as it fits the accepted, unspoken rules of dress. Friends are numero uno. If a teen doesn't have friends, they are in deep doo-doo.

I know what you're thinking; my kid doesn't need friends, she needs God! I agree. Having a bit of faith, or at least a belief system that explains all of life's mystery and confusion goes a long way during adolescence. A number of kids do have faith and beliefs that guide their way. However, those kids are in someone else's family. The adolescent drive for independence makes it difficult to accept things that are neither easily seen nor already internalized as one's own. Even if God has been internalized in your child's life and the values of faith and religion deeply ingrained, it's still a toss-up whether that spirituality will be utilized during years thirteen through nineteen.

I'll give you a personal example of what teenagers face with the developmental dilemma of spirit. Two weeks before I was to be Bar Mitzvahed at age thirteen, I went into the room in my temple where all electronic equipment was kept. After the proper switches were thrown, my tutor and I turned to leave the room. There was a light switch near the door. A small, thin label of red backing and white lettering caught my eye. It was made by one of those label guns where you dial the letter, squeeze the trigger and out spits your sticky tag. It read simply, ETERNAL LIGHT ON/OFF.

You may know that there is an Eternal Light in every temple. In every synagogue the "Light of the Lord," or Ner Tamid in Hebrew, is never allowed to be extinguished. The history of the eternal light goes back to the very beginnings of Judaism. The Eternal Light represents, not only God's presence, but the hopes and dreams of liberation for the Jewish people. This light symbolically lets us know that there's always a place of refuge.

I looked at that switch for a moment and I thought to myself, if I can turn the Eternal Light off, I could turn other things off too. And what proof is there of God anyway? This went on in my head for all of about two seconds. In my very adolescent mind, just like that, my belief in God exploded in spontaneous combustion. It took me another fifteen years or so to start believing again. Faith is always difficult to hold onto. During adolescence, it's that much harder to grasp because a teenager is looking for his or her own answers and the search must unfold without anyone else's proof.

Nobody Ever Understands Teenagers

Once upon a time, when you were a teenager, you searched for answers of your very own. Your struggles were of an ilk never seen by your own parents. For Babyboomers, drugs were synthesized and became commonplace where none were before. Sex and sexuality were played out in ways that shocked the previous generations. Many of you fought to stop a war, and succeeded. Issues of race and injustice were thrust before the eyes of the entire nation.

It was a frightening time for your parents. I'd bet they watched you struggle mightily at times. They probably didn't know if you were going to make it. Still, you survived. And chances are, your parents were as much in the dark regarding your adolescence as you are now during your child's teenage years.

The specific cultural and technological struggles that your daughter faces are different than the struggles you faced. Your son has to sort through images of sex, violence and intense "reality" television that are, no doubt, more sophisticated than the *Mission Impossible* and *Get Smart* you watched. The pipe bombs and semi-automatic weapons of today are significantly more frightening and harmful than the knives and chains of the worst hoodlums of your youth. The amount of information pouring through and available on the Internet had no analogy twenty-five years ago. In fact, the amount of information in the world is doubling every four years or so, and speeding up. It seems to be a very scary place for your child. What if something goes terribly wrong?

Your child will be okay. I can't guarantee this of course, but statistically speaking, he will survive his adolescence just like you did. Carry the faith for your teen that you want him to hold for himself. The important perspective you may be forgetting right now is this: all that's new and frightening to you, your son has cut his teeth on. He has always known MTV and CDs. He's always had the computer in front of him. Just as we were when we pushed against the boundaries of our families and society, your child is, more or less, comfortable with all the noise that we hear as distraction.

I recently saw a photo on the front page of our local paper. Tenth graders were under their desks practicing a "lock down," in case a gunman took over the school. At first, I was horrified and frightened. Then, I remembered having to climb under my desk in elementary and junior high schools. We had to practice "drop and cover" drills to prepare for nuclear war. I wasn't scarred beyond recognition and neither were you. Your teenager won't be either if you help them learn to cope with the hard stuff. Their drills may be different, but the developmental work is exactly the same. Always was, always will be.

Your Teenager Will Be All Right

A song from the musical *Bye-Bye Birdie* exclaims, "Kids! What's the matter with kids today?" The parents in the play didn't understand their teenage children, so they complained about them. It doesn't matter what your teenager does; something will perplex and vex you about what you can't grasp. I once worked with a family that was having trouble with their then seventeen-year-old daughter. The parents, now successful former-hippies were upset and concerned that their child wanted to be, gasp, a cheerleader! This type of parental unrest probably can be traced back to our emergence from the primordial ooze. I can only imagine how upset that fish father was as he watched his teenage boy crawl up on shore. "You're going to live *where*?"

Our inability to know what's up with thirteen- to eighteen-year-olds has little to do with their being bad kids, though they may sometimes act badly. It has little to do with the fact that our society has gone to the dogs, though maybe it has. Your teenager is all right. She lives in a society that generally fears her — that would make anyone angry. She doesn't know who she is yet — that would confuse almost all of us. She is open, for the first time in her life, to the darker and riskier aspects of living — that frightens her. She can't let anyone know about her vulnerabilities because that would keep her a little girl — and that isolates her. Try to understand this teenage struggle for identity. It's time we adults stopped singing along with the parents from *Bye-Bye Birdie*. However, if you must sing, sing about yourself.

Each stage of your child's life triggers
certain memories in your mind.
So your child is now a teenager.
What do you remember of your adolescence?

Chapter 3

When I Was Your Age ...

Who's In Charge Here?

I once took my dog, Juba, to obedience classes. After a couple of weeks, I finally figured out that obedience school had little to do with training dogs. Doggie school was structured to teach dog owners how to behave. Trainers will tell you that, if you want a well-behaved animal, you need to be consistent in your behavior, know what you want, and accept nothing less than full compliance. It was humorous at the beginning of class — all these people thinking they had control over their animals. Sit, stay, heel, wait, come. Commands came furiously, one on top of the other, with little result. Eventually, the two-legged participants in class learned how to command their dogs appropriately, and it worked. Humans, even though we learn slowly, do learn.

Don't get the wrong impression. I'm not suggesting that teenagers are dogs. I'm likewise not suggesting that parents should train their adolescent children with a choke collar and leash. Nothing could be further from the truth. I'm trying to point out that one reaps the greatest rewards when focusing on oneself. In the case of obedience school, most of the dog owners started with the belief that the dog was to be trained. Few understood that it was their own focus that needed the greatest adjustment.

It's a similar situation with your almost-adult children. Your teenager's behavior is such a red herring that it is exceptionally easy to focus on her. *She* needs to learn respect. *She* needs to do her schoolwork. *She* needs not to get arrested. But in my opinion, we *parents* are looking in the wrong direction. I believe the key to understanding your teenager, and doing well with and for her, is to primarily understand yourself and your parenting.

It's upsetting to hear, but the "I know best" method of parenting, the one that has worked for eternity, suddenly stops working when your child enters adolescence. When you parented your infant, positive reinforcement and a stern "no" every now and then were enough. A few years later, very clearly, you told your child what the rules were for doing homework and cleaning his room. Voilá, it worked again. Then puberty arrives. At this point, you stand in front of your teenager, toss out a little positive reinforcement, and tell him the rules. Nothing happens. You shift your weight and try again. Something happens, but it still has no relation to what you wanted. Exasperated, you raise your voice and tell your teenager what's what. The next day he comes home with a pierced nose and an attitude that screams you never, ever understand him! Even if your teen doesn't act out wildly, the change is noticeable. He doesn't follow your lead as he once did. What's the deal?

The Paradox of De-Parenting

The deal is, you don't know best anymore. Just about every teenager who has ever lived knew, or knows, more than his or her parents. A teenager cannot help but rip up the map she was given by you, decide on a new destination, draw a new map, then start the journey on her own. From the perspective of your teenage daughter, your knowledge only delays her adventure. The map you gave her is still valuable, but she just won't let you know it is until she's twenty-two.

Parenting Through The Years: What Works

- ***Infancy and Toddlerhood*** *— Lots of love, positive reinforcement and a stern "no" as needed.*
- ***Childhood Years*** *— More positive reinforcement and love, role modeling, and perhaps, an opportunity for the kids to stretch and take risks while remaining safe.*
- ***Adolescence*** *— Try lots of different things and quit fast when the strategy you choose doesn't work. Take care of yourself.*

Parenting teenagers is a paradox of "de-parenting." It's no longer about taking care of your child and telling him what to do. It's about trying to understand the young man who used to be called "baby," and who now shaves. It's about loving the young woman who needs to be comforted in your arms one moment, and in the next drives off in the family car. It's about taking care of the relationship of adult to almost-adult. This is important. You don't parent your child anymore. You parent the *relationship* with your child.

When our children are infants, toddlers or small children, they need our help. They can't cross the street alone. Getting juice for herself at that age is a major challenge. Going to the bathroom is ... I don't want to talk about it. When our children go to elementary school, and even in the beginning of middle school, they can do much more. Still, they need our help. They can't get across town for soccer practice. And even if a few ten-year-olds know their schedules, most kids don't have the capacity to stay on top of their lives.

Then it changes. Though they won't necessarily clean up afterward, chances are that our teens are able to feed themselves. It's nothing for a teen to hop on the bus and get across town. They may not want to take the bus, but they're able. All the high schools where I live provide day schedulers for the students. Our teenagers know what's happening in their lives. As for the bathroom ... well, I still don't want to talk about it.

Fear is another interesting shift. Most younger kids don't like to be scared. During elementary school, my daughter would not watch certain Disney movies because she knew that an animal was going to get hurt. The theme music from *The X-Files* scared her. Teenagers on the other hand — for whom do you think the *Nightmare on Elm Street* and *Scream* films were made? Blood, guts and gore. Anticipating the monsters' advance. They love it. Weird as it sounds, teenagers like to be frightened.

Truth is, your teenager doesn't need you in the same way anymore. Yes, your wisdom is still worthwhile. Yes, it's fabulous that you have dinners as a family. But your sorta-grown child does not need any of it to survive. They could, most probably, get by on their own. And getting by more on their own is what some of our kids want anyway. That is, in fact, what they are moving toward developmentally. Teenagers can do almost anything they want to do. Sure, there would be hell to pay, but they could do it. Yet they often don't, because, in some unspoken fashion, teenagers know it's best for everyone to follow the leader. You're still the leader. But the control you believe you have over your child is imagined. Pretty terrifying thought — your teenage kids are out of your control. Yikes!

Parenting From a Place of Fear

Did your stomach just do a double back flip? This fear is part and parcel of the experience of parenting teenagers. One of the realities of this time is the ol' separation/individuation thing I talked about previously. As parents, we don't have to separate from them, but we have to let our children grow up and say good-bye to us. What a bittersweet reality. We give and give. We parents learn to give to our children before all else, until our offspring don't want our gifts any longer. I remember my mother, chanting the rhyme, "Sun to sun, sun to sun, a parent's work is never done." She was wrong. At some point, our gifts are no longer desired, then Mom and Dad feel cast aside.

For many parents of teens, every time they greet their emerging adult they are feeling "Au revoir." It's an exceptionally tender time for parents. You catch a glimpse of your daughter and you realize there are only three more years (or two or ...) before she goes off to college. You feel a lump building in your throat. In the next millisecond, you flash on the realization that she doesn't know how to properly do her wash. From your most loving parenting stance, you see how critical it is that she know how to separate colors before she leaves. She won't be able to find happiness without this skill. She can separate from the family later. Isn't your focus always on what she needs to be happy in the world? "Clean your room and do your laundry!" you scream.

What you don't realize is that your commands, most of the time, are your fears disguised as directive caring. Your gut feeling says that if she doesn't have all the skills she needs, if something goes wrong, it's really your fault. You'll have failed her. So you try to teach her everything now. You work at stuffing in all that knowledge and skill before it's too late, before she's gone. That would be fine and dandy if she could accept your help freely, but it just doesn't happen that way. You're worried about your daughter and it's very difficult to see straight when you're carrying this feeling around. Parenting from fear makes it very difficult to make the right decisions for you and your family.

Maximizing Your Parenting Energy

You might feel that I'm over-reacting, and say to yourself that your daughter's room is indeed messy and the laundry, which is her job, simply needs to be done. End of story. With teenagers, it's rarely that simple. A power struggle of epic proportions will commence if you tell your kid what *she* needs to do. Many teenagers, because of the combination of not knowing who they are, of living in a black and white world and being insecure with themselves, will take any direction or request as criticism. "Clean your room" is felt by a sensitive child (that is, all teenagers) to mean "You don't deserve to be loved because you can't get anything right!" A common adolescent response to that feeling is, "You can't tell me how to live! I like my room where I can't find anything. Besides, you don't do anything for me. Why should I do anything for you?!"

I understand the parent who yells at the daughter to do the wash. However, it's never going to be an effective method of building relationship and cooperation between parent and child. Try this: start by anticipating that all your feelings (sadness, anger, surprise, elation, confusion) are going to come up in any interaction with your teenage child. When they do, notice them, put them away for the time being and address them later with a therapist or friend. You will have feelings of all sorts. Don't deny them. But it's better to work them out with someone who will have empathy for you. Generally speaking, your sixteen-year-old has other things on her mind.

Next, take full responsibility for any parental requests. This is a key area in parenting the relationship with your teenager and it's extremely important. The intention and manner with which you ask your child to do anything will mean the difference between her scowling at you or launching a mean, verbal left hook. I'd rather have a dirty look any day. With the clean-your-room-and-do-the-wash example, owning the request would be as simple as saying, "*I* need you to do the wash. It is something *I* want to happen. Thank you for helping *me*." The semantics are critical. "You do the wash and clean your room," as I said, is an insult. Anyone insulting an insecure teen, especially a parent: watch out. "I need your help," though a pain in the tush and an excuse for a groan or two, is not grounds for an attack. The more you focus on your needs with your teenager, the less surface area is available for resistance.

Don't Panic, Don't Worry

Finally, stand firm. As I write this, hurricanes are threatening most of the East Coast. This is a great analogy for families with teens. Be like those brave shop owners who refuse to be evacuated. Adolescence means you will definitely be in for one hell of a storm, but chances are, it won't be the big one that destroys everything. With adolescence, you're going to have to replace a few windows. However, you grew this family into what it is now, and you shouldn't abandon it because of strong winds and six inches of rain. Your son will resist, possibly over and over again. So what? His resistance is not about your success or failure as a parent. Make parenting decisions by acting on what you believe in. Pick your battles. Batten down the hatches. Hold tight.

How To Parent The Relationship

- *Anticipate your own feelings and deal with them away from your child.*
- *Take responsibility for what your want from your child.*
- *Be clear in your intentions. Remember that semantics are important.*
- *Be brave and weather the storm.*
- *Don't try to figure out the "perfect" response.*
- *Don't accept blame or guilt for your teenager's struggles.*
- *Focus on what you, not your child, needs.*

Most parents search for the one correct response and/or consequence to give their children that will miraculously change all negative behaviors. You want your baby to be happy. If he's miserable or makes a mistake, you feel guilty and want to take the blame. Stop looking for the answer. I assure you, this quest will drive you mad. There is no such parenting maneuver. You may not realize it, but you're attempting to figure out what is best for your kid and get her to change. You are falling into the trap of parenting your child, instead of parenting the relationship with your child. You are trying to save her from her pain. I promise, your teen will smell this strategy from four miles away. Your daughter isn't willing to admit to herself or anyone else that she wants to know what you think is best. She doesn't want to become what you want her to become, even if it's exactly what she wants.

So try something. Anything. If you get it right today and your child responds well, tomorrow or next week will bring you a different result. If something does go wrong, have no fear. I have empirical proof that it's not your fault. If you have multiple children, you can see that no two are remotely alike. All children are screwed up in their own unique ways. Any parent out there with two or more children knows this to be true. It can't be your fault. You've done more or less the same thing with each child and each has had different reactions to different issues. The things that go right and wrong for our children occur within the context of a thousand variables. You are but one. Granted, you're the most important one, but only one. Now you can begin to understand the tension that exists in your household. I assure you, you're not alone. Most every parent in my psychotherapy practice shares your pain.

Don't Fear

No matter what you do, sometimes your child will make mistakes and get hurt. You can't keep her totally safe. The adolescent years will always be filled with self-doubt — the developmental deck of cards is stacked. For a teenager, defining himself on his own terms, in a culture that socializes him to fit in makes him a bit nuts. Even the most spectacular, "together" young people struggle with something. Not all children are going to dye their hair purple, listen to gangsta rap or pierce their nipple. Not every one of your children will resist everything you do and/or say and embrace anarchy. However, if they don't, they could instead fall to the other end of the adolescent continuum.

A growing portion of my practice is filled with brilliant, well-adjusted, high-achieving kids who, for a period in their lives, want to die. For whatever reasons, instead of taking their internal turmoil out on their parents and other adults, they turn their commotion in on themselves. They're imploding. They've lost track of the "why" of their achievement. They, too, don't feel normal. They feel trapped. The only way they can imagine to get out of their predicament, for a time, is suicide. Don't worry. There's rarely any need to panic. The kids who are struggling big-time are the ones on the extreme ends of the continuum. The vast majority of teenage children are somewhere safely within three standard deviations from the norm. The adolescent years are simply a no-win time of life. At times, it's miserable for everyone.

And Don't Rescue

The greatest disservice done by our generation of parents has been rescuing our teenage children from any and all pain. Our parents' parents raised their children through the Depression. For most, there was little escape from the hardships of those times. Our parents grew up, made a better life for themselves and, if they could, provided more for us. Yet most of them made us work for what we wanted. They didn't coddle and rescue us. If and when you got in trouble, someone in the neighborhood found out. They told your parents. Then you got in *Big Trouble*. The comedian, Sinbad, talks about getting a whoopin' from every adult between the school where he got in trouble and home. Then he really got his "what's coming." Every adult in the neighborhood paid attention. Trouble was something that brought about pain, and pain taught you a lesson about getting in trouble. That was the standard.

Now we've grown up. We're far more involved in our children's lives than generations before ours. It's a great evolution in parenting. We have quality time. We work on our children's self-esteem. We do prevention instead of intervention. And we have lost one of the great lessons of our parents. Struggle builds character. Hard times teach us that we can survive. A brilliant professor of mine in graduate school looked at it this way: I went to him complaining, "I'm confused. I'm struggling too much!" He would smile his wonderfully wise, sixty-three-year-old smile and say, "Quit bragging." He felt that struggle was the way to growth.

Our generation of adults has, more than ever before, done too much stepping in, deflecting, enabling, speaking for and over-indulging our children. And it shows. We have a large contingent of young people who only know how to wait for someone else to step in and help. When they hit a hard patch in life, many want to quit. Others simply believe that life shouldn't be hard. They resist learning how to cope. These teenagers resist the growth that comes through enduring hardship.

A Shot of Perspective

Every year, I have five or six high-school students tell me that these are supposed to be the very best years of their lives. After I very professionally stifle my laughter, I ask where they get that idea. Ninety percent of the time, teens get the message from their parents. I've met a few of these adults. They never struck me as people who were wildly happy as teenagers or wildly unhappy as adults. I can't figure it out. There is absolutely nothing about going through the teen years that makes them the best.

Okay, so that date with Vicky was the most magical moment of your life. Winning the women's state soccer title still makes you smile. The first time for, well, lots of things was just too cool. But those were isolated incidents. I realize there are actually people reading this that enjoyed themselves during the time their faces broke out, their voices changed or during those six months of Friday nights home alone watching *The Man From UNCLE.* I, too, had good times — even a few great ones. Looking at my whole life though, they were hardly my best years. I know very few people who didn't gain more control over their own lives as they matured. Almost no one who is in charge of his life now can say that he felt better at a time when he had significantly less control. Teenagers are not allowed to have total control in our culture. Why then would you tell someone that his teen years will be better than anything to come?

I'll tell you the reason. Right about the moment this thought enters your brain and/or leaves your mouth, you're feeling out of control with your teenage child. For the moment, you've forgotten what it was like to be a teenager. All you can see is a remarkably selfish young woman doing exactly what she wants. She's certainly not thinking about you one-hundredth as much as you're thinking about her. This reminds you of the good times when you didn't have to work one or more jobs to keep your family fed and sheltered. You didn't worry about anything except having fun when you were a teenager. In fact, when you were her age, you were appreciative of the one night a week you were allowed to go out with friends! On foot! In the snow! Without legs!

Not a very healthy outlook on parenting. The best way to be in control with your teenager is to parent with a healthy perspective. The only way to have a healthy perspective is to take good care of yourself physically, emotionally and spiritually. This is, in fact, exactly what you want for your child — but with most parents, a do-as-I-say-and-not-as-I-do sort of thing. I wonder why?

A Perfect Irony

Most parents of teenagers are, roughly, middle-aged. This, too, is an interesting developmental stage of life. Yes, adults are still developing as well. I find it an unconscious habit of our culture to think that once you're grown up, whatever that means, you don't have to do any more developmental work. You wish. Dr. Erikson believes that our work during this time of life is to make the world a better place. It's the chapter of your life when you truly learn to care about and for others. Simple.

Except, mid-life crisis happens 'round this time. It's no coincidence that many of us enter this challenging time when teenagers are in the house. You're in the process of looking back and reflecting. You can't help but mark how far you've come, and how far you still want to go. You're beginning to recognize, perhaps for the first time, how remarkably mortal you are. It's a time to set goals for the next part of your life and these goals often take you in a very different direction from the path you're currently traveling. It's a time that requires more patience.

These mid-life feelings happen whether or not you're a parent. However, as a parent, you get a few extra roller-coaster rides for the price of admission. Parents remember their own lives through their children. Each stage of your child's life triggers certain memories in your mind. If your child is a teenager, what do you remember about your adolescence? Confusion, fear, anticipation of the unknown, bad dates, insecurity and acne are a few that I recall. You can't help but project some of that old insecurity onto your child when you don't pay close attention to separating your feelings from theirs.

Our teenage kids are doing almost exactly the opposite developmental work that we are. They're freely imagining what might be, not what was. Your son is getting louder and cranking up his Beastie Boys CD. He wants to stay out later. You, on the other hand, are getting more nostalgic, quieter, and going to bed right after *60 Minutes*. You want to be together as a family. Your daughter wouldn't be with you tonight if you paid her. You want to know how your child is doing in school because you care. Your son can't believe you won't stop bugging him. It's his life after all. Teens want freedom while we want a little stability and comfortable shoes. They want excitement today. We're planning for our retirements. What a clash of experience! It's a cruel cosmic joke. God must be somewhere sitting in a comfortable chair, yelling, "Fight, fight!" and laughing uncontrollably.

How can any parent focus on taking care of him or herself during this time of life? It isn't an easy task. How you take care of yourself is up to you, but it must be done. When you're healthy, you're less likely to confuse your teenager's struggles with your own. You'll look at her with love, not fear. Remember what she was like at age four? How about when she graduated from elementary school? Can you even imagine life without her? Think of what she's going to become. Would you trade those future experiences to become an adolescent again? I didn't think so.

A Modest Proposal

I propose that the best way to parent your teenager is to stop trying to run her life. I'm not suggesting you let your almost-adult child do anything she wants, any time she wants. Continue to set limits, encourage healthy risk-talking and decision-making. You absolutely should continue to say no when it makes sense to you. You're in the parenting business for the long haul. No matter what your teenager thinks, this process called family doesn't end when she goes off to Whatsamatta U. Successfully parenting a teenager requires you to stop making your parenting decisions based on what *might* work for your child and start making decisions based on what *will* work for you.

This is counterintuitive to everything you've been taught about parenting. You've always thought of your child first. Mothers can make this behavior an art form. Fathers, while more easily lost in themselves, are pretty good about putting the kiddos first as well. In either case, stop thinking about your teen first. It won't work any more. You can no longer figure out what is best for your teen. They shift and change too fast. They resist too often. As you start to focus on what works for you, within relationship to your child, you'll find yourself interacting with your son about his life. You'll be acting in a developmentally appropriate manner which will allow your fifteen-year-old to be non-defensive. He might feel the love in your conversations for the first time in thirty-three months. Wouldn't you love that?

WHAT DO I BELIEVE?
Part Two

I expect my teenager to:

- *a. Vacuum, mop, dust and trim my toenails.*
- *b. Contribute to the maintenance of our home without being hounded.*
- *c. Just clean her room. Is that too much to ask?*
- *d. Pick up after herself.*

I am happy to support my child financially for extra work:

- *a. Only after she has done all her regular chores.*
- *b. Never! Do I look like a bank?*
- *c. If he needs the money for something constructive.*
- *d. Rarely, I'd rather he get a real job.*

Here are three things you can start today that will help you parent the relationship with your child. First, accept no blame or guilt for problems in your child's life. It does nothing toward helping your struggling bambino take responsibility for his actions, and it puts you smack dab in the middle of his muck. Let him be responsible for his woes. Guilt and blame (yours or his) do not make sense in raising a healthy child. Second, focus on what you need to survive your child's adolescence. Do you like book groups? Exercise? A month-long retreat on a small island off Brazil? Please — you have to take care of yourself. You need your strength. Finally, take lots of credit for his successes. It's okay. When people love him, they love you. Then, bow deeply and thank your parents. It will provide a nice symmetry.

Let's try this out in a real-life example. Suppose you pick up your son from a friend's house one night. You say hello, smell alcohol on his breath and notice that he's more weaving than walking. What do you do? If you're a parent on the verge of a nervous breakdown, you might tell your son how much he's disappointed you. You might let him know you won't be able to trust him for a long time. Certainly, it will be a cold day in you-know-where before he sees that friend again. You let him know that that friend is a bad influence, then ask, "Why don't you have better friends?" Follow this script and your son will be very angry with you. It may drive him to sneak out later that night. You, on the other hand, will be frightened and have a seriously upset stomach. You'll lie awake at three a.m. chanting, "What have I done? Where have I gone wrong?"

Or, you can focus on what you need as a parent. First of all, you'll know not to talk with someone who's under the influence. Have the conversation with your son in the morning when you've cooled off and he has a hangover (advantage, parent!). You can talk about the necessity for mutual trust and respect in the parent-teen relationship. The consequences of his actions can relate to safety, honesty, and self respect. Maybe he'll have to apologize to his friend's parents for behaving that way at their house. Sonny-boy will have to endure a conversation or three on drugs and alcohol with you. You don't have to be heavy-handed. You can give your son responsibility for his actions. After all, he was drunk last night, not you.

Think about what type of relationship you want to have with your teenager. Do you want to be able to talk about the "important stuff" with your child? Remember, he believes he has the right to do his own thing and make his own decisions. His road map is a little hard to read at times, since he's still in the process of drawing it. He may or may not ask for directions. Which parent will he trust enough to share about all that went on last night? Which one does he want to talk with about relationships? With whom would he ask for advice and guidance about a friend who's in trouble? Your teenager will always gravitate toward the interaction behind Door Number 2. Maybe you learn the hard way. Perhaps you enjoy a good fight. In that case, try out the first parenting style. But my suggestion is, don't resist. Just go with the flow. Ease-up, Daddy-O.

Ironically, our struggles during our teen years and our inability to complete the developmental work of adolescence hampers our capacity to pass along the gifts we parents have to share.

Chapter 4

Generational Amnesia

You Are Not Alone

"This is worse than what we did, right?" "I didn't use drugs until I was in college, that's the difference." "Were we ever this bad?" "Did my parents have to go through this?" "I never did this." "My struggles were only with school." "Times are much scarier now than they were when I was a teenager."

Recognize any of these statements? Probably, or you have a version that's all your own. At one time or another, every parent feels this way. Your child, your teen, stomping through what Michael Ventura describes as "extremism — that intense psychic cacophony of adolescence," acts out or pushes against nearly every person close to him. It drives you mad. And I do mean mad, both angry and crazy. Your child's adolescence drives you to pulling your hair out, breaking dishes against the wall, and crying yourself to sleep. It seems as if no one's child has ever pulled at the heartstrings of a parent as sweetly and as painfully as your child is pulling right now. You're so mad you believe that what your kid is doing today has never been done before ... to any other parent. Your child is *really* self-destructing. You've *truly* lost control. That's how mad it feels.

You're wrong. You're not alone. Your pain is not the worst pain. You have not lost total control, nor is you child a sociopath. What your teenager is doing (or may do) may feel different from what happened to you in the last millennium, but the developmental pandemonium is just like the good ol' days. Everything has been done before. The hormones of adolescence have rock and rolled this way forever.

The feeling that "it's surely worse now, here" is what I call Generational Amnesia. It's the inability of "this" generation of parents to recognize that what's happening now has happened before, and that it will happen again. Teenagers in the 1990s, you and me at age seventeen, the thousands of generations that came before us — we have all been just as violent, just as angry, just as passionate, just as wonderful, just as curious, just as rebellious and just as interested in the darker side as the kids we're parenting today.

I read a newspaper article that detailed a study suggesting that teenagers have a bad reputation among adults. I assume this was a costly and statistically reliable investigation. The findings of this study were (1) adults believe teenagers lack good manners (2) adults believe teens to be dangerous and (3) adults don't want to hang with their adolescent brethren. Well, DUH! Of course, that's the way adults see teenagers. It's the way we've always seen them, at least since early Greek and Roman times. Aristotle believed that if the teens of his time were the future, then society was in serious trouble. He felt that teens were not serious enough about community, helping others, or scholarship. Aristotle also believed that teens drank way too much. Every generation before us has been worried about its teenagers. Why should we be different?

We have never been able to immunize parents against the particular societal affliction of disliking the young. The malady is always with us. The identifying symptom appears whenever teenagers, wearing something hip, come within three hundred yards. If a parent is older than thirty-five, her face will turn red and she'll break into a narrative which includes the phrases "When I was your age ..." and "Things sure have changed since my youth!" This speech pattern is accompanied by a specific amnesia which blocks out any knowledge of developmental behavior, the afflicted's memory of her own teenage years and all historical perspective. This insidious form of memory loss is rooted in the fact that parenting is always reinvented in our culture. When we become parents, it's for the first time. Our kids become teenagers for the first time. We haven't been taught about all those who parented before us. Students of history or not, the parenting experience is brand new to each of us. We don't remember, and that makes it easier for adults to not feel compassion for anyone who is thirteen to nineteen years old.

May I See Your License, Ma'am?

I had a conversation with a friend a number of years back. He was playing with the idea of licensing parents. It seemed only right. In order to operate a four-door, 2,000-pound weapon of destruction legally, you have to go through a fair amount. You need to complete a driver's education class (which includes viewing the classic *Blood on the Highway)*, obtain a learner's permit, survive being instructed on the correct way to parallel park by father, then take written and highway drivers' tests. Only then can you get a driver's license. So, at sixteen or thereabouts, you're a legal, albeit mediocre, driver. The police can't stop you, as long as you obey the traffic laws.

On the other hand, anyone can become a parent. Some of us have the good fortune to meet and recognize the love of our life. We court one another. Then, we marry and, in due time, conceive. Others go a less traditional route. Whether single, married or in another type of committed relationship, some have the gift of adopting the child of their dreams. But all anyone really has to do is find someone to have sex with, not use contraception (either on purpose or out of hormonal stupidity), and have the soon-to-be mother (and, hopefully the father) decide that she wants this baby more than anything else in her life. You're a parent in no time flat.

Requirements For

Driving	*Parenting*
• *Driver's Ed. class*	• *Sex*
• *Six months with a learner's permit*	
• *Fifty hours driving with an adult*	
• *Driver's training class*	
• *Written and highway tests*	

If Something Goes Wrong

Driving	*Parenting*
• *Traffic tickets*	• *Therapy for the kids*
• *Fines*	
• *Loss of license*	

None of these scenarios require parenting classes. There are no required child development classes. You don't have to be mentored about the trials and tribulations of parenting by a sweet, kind couple. Nothing really prepares you for what lies ahead, except your own experience with your parents.

That might not be bad if you had perfect parents. Did you? I thought not. A great truism is: "Your parents will mess you up at one time or another, in one way or another, and you'll remember it forever." It happens because our parents became parents just like we did. No classes or information. No experience. They walked into the same black hole their parents did before them.

Ain't No Such Thing as a Perfect Parent

Yet it wouldn't matter if we had perfect parents. We move through childhood with the vision and memory of a child, not a parent. When we're young, few of us say to ourselves, "That's just what I want to do when I'm a daddy. I better write that down." We experience the familial equivalent of "those who refuse to learn from history are condemned to repeat it." That's why, when you yell at your son, "I brought you into this world and I can take you out!" or "You're crying? I'll give you something to cry about!" your stomach clenches into a gigantic knot and you think to yourself, "Oh my God, I've become my father!"

When we're children, it's nearly impossible to see the world from our parents' perspective. I have such a clear memory of my daughter being born. Not until that very moment — in that instant when the color blue took on a different and richer hue, the smell of fresh cut grass became stronger, the taste of a strawberry sweetened — did I have a perspective other than as an individual and a child. At that moment, under the full moon, I developed the perspective of a parent, perhaps primarily. In the blink of an eye I better understood my parents' joys and sorrows. I was, in a child's breath, just like my dad, just like my mom.

Still, it was very difficult for me to allow my parents to help me parent after Zoë was born. I had to learn it all on my own. I resisted their advice. I wanted space alone with my new family. I know I'm not the only one who's taken this stance. Though some of us accept and appreciate our mothers' gifts of experience, too often we, the children, like adolescents, want to do it our own way.

In Western culture, we've done a poor job of transmitting knowledge about parenting. The problem lies, first, in how we ask about what came before us and, second, how parents share their knowledge. To start with, people love to share trauma. Watch complete strangers or close friends approach a pregnant woman. Out come horror stories about how labor was their most painful experience ever, that it took 237 hours for the baby to come out, and that their child weighed sixty-eight pounds at birth. Okay, but still — every time a first-born comes out of a mother's womb, it's like the first birth *ever*. Most stories told to expectant parents contain value judgments and projected feelings. It's better to pretend you haven't been given any information at all than to take in this muck of advice.

As your child grows, you remember for the first time in many years what it was like when you were younger. Your memories of adolescence are often tumultuous; intense ups and downs, confusion and anger. During your baby's childhood, unless there were some exceptionally tough times in your family, you have good memories of holidays, birthdays and rituals. In your child's early years, because few of us remember infancy, you ask your parents to tell you what you were like as a child. You ask that question, in fact, any time the going gets rough in your parenting.

It's the wrong question to ask. Our childhood memories are the wrong ones to focus on as we try to parent well. Instead of asking what we were like, we need to ask our mothers and fathers what *they* were like as parents. Parenting is not about us as kids. Our memories of childhood are not necessarily happy. This is why John Bradshaw made it so big, healing all those inner children. As Jack Nicholson said in *As Good As It Gets*, "Some people had happy childhoods with picnics and noodle salad, just no one in this car." Parenting is about us as adults, as parents.

A Great Big Straight Line

Look at your child and then ask what your parents think they did right and wrong. What would they have done differently given the opportunity to do it all over again? What would they do exactly the same way because of the magic it produced for you, for them and for the family? As the parent of teenagers, you need help and support. Lots of it. Knowing what went south or north for your folks could help your journey. Ask them. I promise, you won't be expelled from the garden if you eat from your parents' tree of knowledge.

When my daughter was a very wise three-year-old, she and I were driving around on errands. Our ride was quiet. As we pulled into a parking space in front of the shoe store, Zoë turned to me. "It's like a great, big, giant line," she began. I didn't have the slightest idea what she meant. "Well, you have a mom, right? And she has a mom, and her mom had a mom, and on like that. It's a great, big, straight line."

Too often though, we children/parents sever that long line. It is, for many reasons, too difficult to ask parents to share what they know. It's even harder to receive it without invitation. For many of us, when we look to our families, and especially our parents, we feel stuck in a snapshot from a bad family vacation. We remember being and feeling a child. We see our parents as they were then — Mom with big teased hair and Dad with baggy plaid pants

We don't want them to tell us what to do anymore. We want to be independent and grown-up. Unfortunately, this simple desire for independence from our families is an indictment. It indicates that we haven't yet reached freedom. It's like a New-Age nightmare. What we want, we don't have. "Stop wanting and you *will* have" our gurus proclaim. But we do want. HELP!!

I'll Do My Work, You Do Yours

To parent a healthy, sane teenager we need to help our child complete her developmental work. In order to do that, we're required to do the same for ourselves. Remember what Erik Erikson suggested — if your child gets bogged down in one stage of development, that stage and the next one become difficult to conclude. In middle adulthood, you should be concerned with such issues as justice for all people and the kind of world you'll leave for your children. If you avoid this developmental work, your behavior will inevitably go to one extreme or the other.

An illustration of one extreme: Mom starts wearing her daughter's miniskirts and platform shoes, and dates the twenty-seven-year-old she met at the health club. Dad starts driving a sports car and dates the twenty-seven-year-old's younger sister. Or the other extreme: Mom and Dad start thinking about how short the rest of their lives will be. They get depressed and lethargic. Eventually, even at age forty-nine, you have to grow up. At a young seventy-two, Dr. Erikson felt, "A person does best at this time to put aside thoughts of death and balance its certainty with the only happiness that is lasting: to increase, by whatever is yours to give, the good will and higher order in your sector of the world."

Your kids have to do their own developmental work, which is hard-wired into every cell of their beings. However, it's your son's work to struggle with his particular stage of development. You get to work on your own very different developmental stage. If you don't do yours, he probably won't do his. It's a bit like that oil filter commercial. "You can pay me now, or pay me later." Many of our parents didn't know how to help us through our adolescent anguish. They couldn't because they hadn't worked through their own. Ironically, our struggle during our teen years, and our inability to complete the developmental work of adolescence has hampered our ability to receive our parents' gifts now. And it hampers our ability to pass along our own gifts to our teenagers.

Growing up, I was known as Johnnie. Everyone called me Johnnie, and it was o.k. with me. At some point during my fourteenth year, I decided that I was to be called John. Johnnie was a kid's name and I was no longer a little kid. My friends, of course, had no trouble with the transition. I had to punch Michael in the arm once, but after that he never made that mistake again. My family had a lot more trouble. They called me Johnnie over and over again for the next three years. I became militant. When anyone called me by the wrong name, the culprit received eighty verbal lashes. I would scowl and punish the Johnnie-sayer for days.

Then, at some point, I changed. I don't mind being called Johnnie anymore. I rather like it now, to tell you the truth (though my mother and sister are still gun-shy thirty years later when they call me Johnnie). I grew up and out of my adolescence on that one. With some other issues though, I didn't make it out so clean. We're all like that.

We grow out of some of our old stuff easily. Other issues linger just out of sight, in such a way that we can't identify them, but still smelly enough to know that something is bothering us. A therapist I respect says that our unresolved issues are out in the hallway, doing push-ups and getting stronger. They're waiting for the time when they can cause more trouble. If you don't want to be surprised and overpowered by your childhood stuff, you need to identify and deal with your old problems.

These old, goopy issues clog you up and keep you from being a healthy human being. Though some of your patterns may be decades old, when they go unnoticed, they constantly intermingle with today's experiences. Every memory of your family, and your place in it, is now a part of the way in which you deal with your children. It takes practice to realize that these feelings are not adult thoughts. They represent that adolescent "you" bathed in old anger, confusion and angst. Unless you pay attention, your old patterns will have the run of your brain and befuddle the way you act and feel now.

So uncover them. Look at your behavior with the understanding of an adult and not the confusion of a child. Figure out how to come to terms with your issues. Be creative. Remind yourself that you're all grown up and that you don't have to play out the same old patterns. Work on new, innovative, positive ways of dealing with your family of origin. It's important to recognize the old goop, but let it go. Though once a tool for survival, these thoughts and feelings no longer serve you.

Have you heard of the statement "It's never to late to have a happy childhood"? Well, this is your opportunity. I'm not talking about "healing your inner child." As far as I'm concerned, we'd all be better off if we could find a really great inner babysitter and let our adult go out for a night of dinner and dancing. I am talking about separating your experience as a teenager from being the parent of a teenager. When you do this, you become a fine-tuned, well-oiled, parenting machine.

This type of parent is confident. She hears what her children have to say without getting defensive. This type of parent is flexible. She's open to suggestions, even from *her* parents. Chew on that one for a moment. A child open to the suggestions of a parent. A child available to an elder's wisdom. It's exactly what you wish for your reticent sixteen-year-old. Now there's symmetry! Physician, heal thy self!

Warning! Explicit Lyrics

Have you noticed that you're no longer able to understand two-thirds of the lyrics in the music to which your teenager is listening? Almost overnight (at the age of thirty-eight years and two months to be approximate), you don't understand a word of what your hearing. It doesn't matter whether the music is Jay-Z's rap, Smashmouth's ska or Limp Bizkit's hard rock. It all sounds like yelling over loud, synthesized white noise.

When it comes to music, most parents believe that their kids' generation is ridiculous. For example, I've noticed that the category name for mainstream rock and roll is "alternative." And I hate Generation X's award show, the MTV Video Music Awards. Every Pop Star dresses down in glittery grunge and chews gum while giving "ups" (that means thanks) to their posse (friends), while a Rock Star flips off somebody else as a mandatory gesture of rebellion. Why can't they all realize that there are some times when dressing up and acting appropriately is a good idea?! What's wrong with them?! When I was their age ... Sorry. I became my father for a moment. I couldn't stop myself.

Music is one area where parents lose perspective, and sometimes their tempers. Parents worry a lot about the music their kids are hearing. They wonder how, or if, angry lyrics or sexually explicit words will affect children to act out in ways they can't control. Recently, a parent of a fourteen-year-old client asked me whether I was worried about the effects of gangsta rap, like the type his son listened to. He joked nervously about whether I was packing a piece to protect myself from violent, rampaging youth. I assured him as I'll assure you: I'm not worried.

Look back one generation to our adolescence. We grew up to rock and roll, the music of Tune In, Turn On and Drop Out. It didn't lead to, but *grew out of* the Summer of Love. It didn't organize, but *spoke for* the peace movement. Our parents were frightened and confused. Where would that music lead us to? Look back another generation. The Big Band sound was wild. All that movin' and touchin' while dancing. It was so racy. Racy enough to make a return in the late 1990s. The Cherry Poppin' Daddies and other groups brought back zoot suits and swing dancing. Go back again. In the 1920s, the Lindy and the Charleston were absolutely scandalous.

Every group of almost-adults creates something new, something that can be feared and misunderstood by parents. Music, like parenting, is recreated in every generation. In his book, *Letters at 3 am*, Michael Ventura quotes Michael Corcoran, a rock critic, who speaks about the music of adolescence:

> *It's rebel music, soul music, kids' music. It understands what parents and teachers don't, that puberty is not about hair or pimples or cracking voices; it's a beast, a demon. It's a beautiful rage that wants to belong and sometimes only can through dumb, simple, angry music. Rap doesn't incite violence, nor does metal. It stirs deep emotions that sometimes get out of hand. It ignites the same spirit that makes us fall in love, have children and believe in God.*

You might be able to control the airwaves in your home, but the rest of the world is tuned in and listening. What your daughter listens to is mostly out of your control. You can't stop her friends, or your friends, or the stores she walks into from playing what you worry about. It doesn't mean that your daughter is out of control. Tipper Gore and her explicit lyric warnings won't save your little girl, because she doesn't need to be saved. Look at the last line of what Corcoran said. The music ignites their spirits. Look where our rebel music brought us. Most of us have grown up all right. We're very much a part of what Henry Fairlie termed "The Establishment." Our music didn't destroy us. It helped us grow up. It'll do the same for your child.

We're Not in Kansas Anymore, Toto

It's not just the music, though. Everything about today's world frightens you. What about the violence? One parent I work with is worried because her son carries a baseball bat in the trunk of his car — just in case. Then there are guns and school shootings in Colorado, Oregon and elsewhere. Teen suicide is a horrific reality. And it's not just the violence either.

Look at the small things. Our children are spending untold hours in Internet chat rooms. They don't spend as much time outside. A number of years ago, a television commercial promoted a brand-new, interactive video game. You hooked a pad to your computer and ran in place on it, competing against a sixteen-bit techno-runner. I laughed. I cried. I went outside and exercised. Technology in general, speeds things up. And, our kids are too busy. When will they have time to just be kids? What about the Materialism of this era? If parents are not careful, the cost of getting their teens the "right look" can cost an arm and a leg.

Here's the thing. All that other scary stuff is not so different from the music. What's going on nowadays has been going on always, if you're eighteen. Your children have never known life without Sportscenter on ESPN. The World Wide Web is simply an understandable next step for someone who was taught about gigabytes and CD-ROM drives in elementary school. For your child, "old school" is not where you went to college. It's five years ago. Sexual identity is simply a part of who your teen is. It's not strange and scary to your teenager. At least, not like it's scary for us.

To a parent, a lot of now is new and, therefore, frightening. I have this vivid memory of riding my bike with my friend to buy used records. My daughter only knows compact discs. I had to take a typing elective (on a typewriter, by the way) in high school. My daughter doesn't need to. She's been typing on our Mac and in the school computer lab since kindergarten. My daughter can easily imagine a car that drives itself. These cars are in research and development labs all over the world right now. In my childhood, that concept was science fiction.

The world in which our children are growing up is foreign to us. What you don't know frightens you. Generational amnesia is simply a shot of xenophobia with a generation gap chaser. We're unfamiliar with so much of our children's world, and it makes us afraid. When groups in power feel frightened and vulnerable, they attack. That's what goes on with adults and parents with teenagers. We are trying to destroy what we don't understand. You'll find that if we give thisgeneration a chance, they'll come in peace. They'll even want their parents to live long and prosper.

Remembering the Present

Don't be frightened. I have the vaccine for generational amnesia. To be cured, all you have to do is say the following outloud, three times daily, with feeling: "Teenagers are fabulous. They're curious and alive, vibrant and passionate, feisty and searching. Teenagers are struggling, sometimes ungracefully with very little help, toward adulthood. I know that my teenager is not the highest evolutionary form of our species, so how might I support him?" You will feel much better in the morning. That's it. It's really that simple. In your mind's eye, create a new vision of your teenager and the rest will fall into place.

WHAT DO I BELIEVE?
Part Three

My teenager should be back in the house:

a. *By six every night. Do you know how scary it is after dark?*
b. *Dinner time each night unless we communicate differently.*
c. *By 5 a.m. the next morning.*
d. *Once a month in order to get more money from me.*

When my teenager uses the Internet:

a. *She's only allowed to surf Mr. Wacky's Wild World of Childhood Fun.*
b. *Any site that passes the parental filter I installed.*
c. *Any site she chooses. I trust her.*
d. *This thing has other uses besides as a decorative paper weight?*

I know, I don't live with your child. I know that you love your kid a great deal and she's still impossible. It seems to be a trap or a trick: if only you deal with your own feelings, everything can change for the better. Of course, no matter what you do, your child's actions may still say "The hell with you." All I can say is, hope is of the utmost necessity at this stage of parenting. Just changing your belief and attitude toward your teen may seem thin as a solution, but then what's the alternative? A federally mandated "War on Teens"? Please, don't take adolescent children so seriously. Try to enjoy your daughter's indomitability. Believe your wild child will come through her adolescence just fine.

I was on a subway in West Berlin eight years before the Berlin Wall came down. I was riding with a friend who was an artist. A group of about twelve hardcore punks entered the car. All sported black leather clothing, chains, steel-toed army boots and brightly colored mohawks. You could see the other adults on the train clutch their purses and lower their eyes. Everyone else was afraid, but my friend struck up a conversation. She loved their hair. It was so artistic and beautiful. She wondered aloud whether it took a lot of work. My friend wanted to know what they used for a stiffening agent (gelatin or white glue, by the way). We talked to these teens for almost an hour. There was no need for anyone to be afraid. These teens weren't out for blood. They were friendly and interesting.

For a moment, try to envision what you were like at your adolescent's age. You wanted someone to see you fully, even through your tough facade. Remember? Trust your child. Your son knows the world in which he lives. His fears aren't so much about what's happening around him, but about his inner turmoil. Your daughter's anxiety, good or bad, is pretty much the same as your struggles as a teenager.

If you didn't work through your adolescent issues, I'll bet good money your teen is struggling with exactly the same issues today. Deal with your stuff. Trust your parenting. The values you provided for your child when she was younger are there. You don't need to try to stop your teenager from being or doing anything. Learn to be a martial artist here — maintain your balance. Get out of the way of their anger, but respect their work. Help them grow up. If you cared deeply when your teenager was a small child, you'll both survive her adolescence. Don't forget, this will all be over in about fifty years.

When you figure out what you believe and why,
the load you carry as a parent will lighten.

Chapter 5
Own Your Muffin

Take a Picture, Why Don't Ya

Right now, I want you to try an exercise that will help you considerably over the next few years. Although it won't produce abs of steel, it will make your heart and soul quite a bit stronger. Find a comfortable, quiet place to sit. Turn off the phone, the stereo and any other distractions. Now, in your mind's eye, create and hold a vision of your teenage child. If the first image that comes to you is your son enraged, saliva flying from his mouth as he screams about how he'd be better off on his own, try again.

Take a deep breath or two, let go of your fears, and see your child with your heart: eyes shining brightly, mind working soundly, with good friends, a solid family connection, doing well in school. Create as full a picture of your almost-adult as you're able, and then hold it until a smile lights upon your lips. Imagine the relationship you have with that young man. Notice how the two of you communicate and get along. Conjure up the relaxed manner in which conflicts are resolved. Feel what it's like to share each other's love. Envision your child's values. Isn't it grand?

Whatever else you take from this book, remember this image. Seeing and feeling the picture of your child, happy and healthy, is a critically important key to your family's happiness and health. Seeing your child from this place of love will allow you to reach him more effectively than from any other place, regardless of the situation. When you parent from the heart, your child will be able to take in more of the love and guidance you offer and use it for their growth toward independence.

Nightmare on Your Street

Most parents spend much too much time loving their children from a position of worry and fear. Recently, I had a conversation with three colleagues who have close to sixty years combined experience working with teenagers. All three are good at what they do. They're confident, clear and strong when it comes to dealing with teens in the school environment. However, when it came to talking about their own teens and their own parenting, you could touch their fear. Tension is not the only thing so thick it can be cut with a knife. One parent/teacher talked about older boys "sniffing around" her pretty daughter after the first day of school. Another was concerned about her child's preparation for high school. They all volunteered their personal tales of teenage parenting terror. There was enough distress for everyone present to have second and third helpings.

Every parent has her own particular fears for her child. For you, it might be seeing your daughter depressed and unable to cope with life. You might shudder when imagining your son lazy, without a high school diploma, working a menial job. You might even envision the nightmare of bodily harm coming to your sweet teen. No matter how hard any of us try, we can't avoid these fears. They creep in through our unconscious. They hang around our hearts and souls regardless of what's going well in our lives. We're unable to escape fear's presence. We can, though, avoid the effects of our fears.

As you parent a teen, fear comes at you from numerous directions. It would be enough to just contend with the world speeding up and changing in ways that are foreign to your experience. And it would be enough to wrestle with the fears that come from not getting much, if any, loving feedback from your daughter. But no, you also have to endure the fears that are a result of the direct confrontations with and/or misbehaviors of your unsweetened, seventeen-year-old woman-child. You worry about outside forces. You feel disconnected. You watch your adolescent acting wildly. You're afraid. Then you parent out of desperation, worry and fear.

Your daughter knows when this is happening. She can feel it. Your worries don't make sense to your not-so-little girl. She feels certain that she knows what she's doing. Everyone else her age is doing the same thing. In her own eyes, she's fine. Tension builds between the two of you. You worry more. This is experiencing the effects of your fear. Most parents don't realize how their feelings and intentions affect the relationship between parent and teenage child. But those feelings do affect what happens in your household, big time.

You Gotta Have Faith

Go back to the visioning exercise. See your child happy and healthy. Stay there as long as necessary to return your blood pressure to normal and your pulse rate to 60ish. You won't have to stay in this relaxed state until your daughter leaves for college, because just a few minutes of positive thinking can put you in a position to appropriately respond to your teenager's predictably ridiculous behavior and anger. From a place of trust and faith, set a limit for your daughter. Ask and expect your teen to do what you need. Explain to her what you're doing and why. Your little one may still battle, but you'll be far more effective when you act from a position of belief and understanding.

Parents often come to my practice carrying the weight of great sadness and guilt. These folks are worried about losing or having lost the connection with their teenager. Each one is fearful that another parent or person has disturbed the already-tentative relationship with their adolescent. I promise, even when another person is in the picture, it's not true that the connection with your teen has been severed. As my father says, maybe you're just having a bad decade.

Keeping the Faith for Your Teenager

- *Imagine your child happy, healthy and well-grounded.*
- *Treat your teen like he was the child in your imagination.*
- *Look for signs of your son's intelligence everywhere.*
- *Compliment your teen on anything he does right.*
- *Rid yourself of guilt.*
- *Know exactly what you believe.*

Your family will always be your family. You're in it together for the long haul. Wounds can and will heal. If only you remain present and available, your child will come back. However, loving your child is not enough — you have to maintain the faith that your adolescent will grow up and be just fine.

There's no secret to keeping the faith. Just act as though what you want to be true *is* true — even with evidence to the contrary. Act as though your bratty daughter *will* pull through and be okay. Start by practicing the exercise I gave you at the beginning of this chapter. Imagine your daughter to be happy and healthy. Then, place that overlay on the transparency that is your emerging adult. Look carefully and treat her as if she's the child of your heart and soul. The more you do the exercise, the more you will notice your teen actually is the person you hoped she'd be. You'll be treating her with respect and high expectations, and she'll respond accordingly.

Next, pay close attention to any actual signs that confirm the existence of intelligent life in your child, and that attest to the connection between you and your almost-adult. That is, look and listen everywhere for positive feedback about your fourteen-year-old pain-in-the-tush. Ask his friends' parents how he acts with them. Talk to teachers and insist they tell you at least two good things about your son. Compliment him on anything he does that smacks of goodness.

Our society has been preset to look for the negative in teens, and teens do show adults negative behaviors. It's common for a sixteen-year-old to become his family's identified problem, but if you want your son to be something other than a problem, you must see him as a positive force in the world. There is more to keeping the faith, of course, but not much.

Grab the Pebble, Grasshopper

You also have to rid yourself of guilt about how you're parenting your teenager. No big deal, really. The most effective way to de-guilt yourself is to figure out exactly what you believe about every little thing you anticipate your teenager experiencing. Figure out how he might push you as a parent. Pull out a highlighter and use it on that part about guilt. It's important. You also have to understand the why of whatever stand you take.

I promise, when you figure out what you believe and why you believe it, the burden of parenting a teenager will lighten. The clouds will part, the sun will shine, and birds will sing. Maybe that's a bit over the top, but your experience *will* be easier. Plus, you'll aid your teenager in his developmental work. Your clarity and solid belief system will give your son a solid foundation from which to leap. He can begin the process of becoming the person he wants to become. But wait, there's more! If you act now, because you'll be parenting from a balanced stance, when the little tyke hits you with his best adolescent angst and anger, he won't knock you off kilter.

Knowing what you believe as a parent assists you in assuming the martial arts stance I mentioned previously. If you've never done Karate, don't worry. Flash back to old *Kung Fu* reruns. Kwai Chang Caine was always centered in his existence. Part of this inner peace came from knowing completely that he was connected to the All. With Parent Fu, a black belt mother or father knows absolutely that they are now, and always will be, connected to the child and the family. No amount of anger, action or distance can lessen the connection. Don't doubt your powerful family ties. When you're not fearful about losing your baby, you won't act out of fear. You won't do anything desperately.

WHAT DO I BELIEVE?
Part Four

It is important for my teenager to have dinner with the family:

- a. *Every night.*
- b. *Every weeknight.*
- c. *One night per week.*
- d. *Rarely, if ever. I never did like that kid anyway.*

I want my teen to be able to sleep at a friend's house:

- a. *One night per weekend.*
- b. *Every weekend night.*
- c. *Whenever they damn well please.*
- d. *Rarely, if ever. I never did like that kid anyway.*

I believe my teenager should have alone time away from family:

- a. *As often as he/she chooses.*
- b. *Alone time? Is my child depressed?*
- c. *Three times per week.*
- d. *Rarely, if ever. I never did like that kid anyway.*

Parent from your heart and within your beliefs and, I assure you, things will be different with your teen. Times won't always be easy, but they will be better. Therefore, Grasshopper, it's time for you to grab the pebble from the palm of my book and figure out exactly what it is you believe.

If there's more than one of you parenting your sometimes-out-of-control teenager, talk together about all the areas where you and your teen will dance. It will be more comfortable for you and better for your teen if you and your partner agree on practically everything. Talk it over with your partner and come to some well-conceived positions from which to parent. When you know what you believe, you can calmly and clearly respond to her without losing your cool (and you won't lose the valuable martyr points you've earned up to this point).

Your Work Is ...

Your little girl has to grow up and decide who she is and how she wants to operate in the world. You have to live with the effects and consequences of your parenting actions. In order for either of these to happen, you have to believe fully in what you do. You have to understand why you're doing whatever it is you're doing. For me or any other expert to instruct you on what choices to make in order for you to be an excellent parent is simply absurd (besides, all the glory goes to you this way). Don't resist. Figure out what *you* believe in. I promise, you'll thank me someday when you're older. I'm sorry you don't like what I am saying, young lady. When you write a book, you can say whatever you want. Gosh, parenting cliches even work on parents!

In one way or another, your daughter will work hard at creating her adolescent space. She might tattoo something you'd rather not know about. She might date a convict. She could do poorly in school, develop an eating disorder, or try one of a million other variations on the theme. Those are all her choices. Never yours. Your work is to decide how you want to parent her. Your work is to find out who you want to be as a parent taking care of your sometimes-snotty teenager. Do you want to be nosy? Bossy? Controlling? Open? Sharing? Loving? Some combination of the above? These are all your choices.

Recently, my daughter didn't feel well and really wanted to stay home from school. For all sorts of good reasons, my wife and I told her she had to go. Zoë did not concur. Our decision made her angry. She wouldn't eat breakfast nor do most of the other things that probably would have helped her feel a little better. Her disappointment led her to scream, resist and slam doors in our general direction. She insisted that I didn't love her.

In the process of getting her out of the house and off to school, my feelings were hurt and there were moments when I was pretty uncertain that I was making the correct parenting choice. The fact that

I had done the work before that morning to know what I believed to be correct about staying home from school saved me. In the face of her anger, I could fall back on what I believed, and let her be frustrated. Her attitude and actions did nothing to change mine, negatively or positively. I was in charge of the situation and could respond creatively. I didn't have to punish her for her fervor, nor cave in from her pressure. Granted, it helped immensely that my wife was supporting me every step of the way. Still, if I hadn't known what I believed, I would have been looking to a screaming child for direction. Not a good choice.

WHAT DO I BELIEVE?
Part Five

With regards to vacations and family trips, my teen will:

a. *Always go with us.*
b. *Be with us, but he/she can bring a friend.*
c. *Not be with us given a special opportunity.*
d. *Shut up and get in the car.*

My teenager needs to help with his/her younger siblings:

a. *Whenever I say so.*
b. *On occasion, when we both agree.*
c. *Never. My kids are my responsibility.*
d. *Stay away from your brother and drop the knife please.*

Just Yours, Not Theirs

When you spend more time trying to retain control of your teenager (even for the best of reasons), rather than helping your not-so-little one figure out that she can shape her own life, the revolution begins. I don't know how it'll play out, but I promise, you'll feel it. The reality of parenting a teenager is this: no matter how you try to boost your son up to a better life, part of him will resent it. And you'll hear about it. It will serve you and your adolescent man-child all the more if you teach him a simple lesson. You may not be able to change the world, but you may change your own life.

I have very little control over anyone else, especially my family. Sometimes others respond positively to what I say and do, while at other times they aren't so gracious. Generally, my attempts to control my daughter and partner (or anyone else) are rebuffed. And though I can enlist other's help and support to move the metaphorical mountains in my life, I have learned that I have no control over how the people in my life meet and join me. The help and love others accept from or offer to me comes from within them. It's their will, their choice to give and receive.

It's the same for you, and it's the same for your teenager. No matter how much control you want or think you have over your adolescent child, it's illusory. Your teenager may not know this to be so. Chances are your teen thinks she has little control over her life. She's partly correct, and she's partly mistaken. That's her problem, though.

Thinking about who you are as a parent will change your life, and your teenager's as well. Identifying the clear framework of your parenting values will help you to move out of the way of your teenager's constant pushing. Own your muffin and you'll be better able to accept your teenage children as they are. Adolescents often get approval for what they do, but rarely feel accepted for who they are. Knowing yourself will help you love and accept your teens as they are. They'll like that. So go forth and figure. Find out what you believe. Do me a favor though — don't get stuck in one way of thinking. Be creative. Have fun. Change your mind. Don't take it personally.

Honoring a moment with reflection and celebration can bring great strength to the next moment.

Chapter 6

Between Two Rocks, A Hard Thing

Smile and Say Cheese

Think back a few years. Remember when you first got pregnant? I don't want to know how, just when. You found out and the rest of your life flashed before your eyes. In a nanosecond, you imagined holding your baby, watching her walk for the first time, playing catch with the little tyke, walking your daughter to school. Out of no experience popped thousands of happy memories yet to be created. Maybe you waited three months before you told everyone else. Friends and parents screamed with delight. When Mom started to show, complete strangers approached to congratulate her and offer unsolicited advice.

You started planning for the new family member. Your friends threw you a party to mark this most remarkable of occasions.

Birth — congratulations! After you get over the miracle, you settle in for a life of exhausted bliss. Everything is new again. Everything is "for the first time" in your family. Cameras click and videos roll to capture first poop, smile, roll-over, solid food, steps. You name it, it goes in the photo album. First holidays, first birthday party, first words, the alphabet song. Then, your little baby goes off to school.

Starting school is a very strong memory for me — Zoë, my wife, Jeffy, and I walked hand in hand in hand to the elementary school. We played on the playground for a couple of minutes, then the classroom door swung open to a brave, new world for our daughter. We walked Zoë in, wished her luck and left. Two steps out the door, Jeffy and I were in tears. I had to convince Jeffy that we couldn't pull our daughter out of school until she had been there for at least twenty minutes. That transitional moment was wrenching! Our family went out to dinner to celebrate that night. Chicken fingers and milkshakes, I think.

On and on we grew. Every new event recorded for posterity and marked as important. But as our children grow older and a little more private we often don't, or can't, mark the passages as easily. I have a good friend whose menstrual cycle started when she was in the fifth grade. She didn't tell her mother for another three years, and her mom never asked. My friend managed to hide from her parents the fact that she had physically begun to be a woman. She went through perhaps the most important physical change that young women experience and she did it privately, by herself. It makes me sad that she wasn't welcomed into her maturity more openly. It surprised me even more to find a number of my other women friends had experienced this as well.

With boys, pubic hair appears. By this time, your son is probably not letting you near him unless he's fully clothed. He locks the bathroom door when he showers. He addresses you loudly and aggressively if you attempt to enter his room while he's changing. A couple of parents in my practice haven't seen their fifteen-year-old boys' bodies for years. They can only assume that their sons have started to show body hair, but they don't know for sure.

Most of us try to respect our children's privacy. With milestones other than the physical, we also back off. We don't take as many pictures or videos. Family celebrations are pared down to the traditional ones; Thanksgiving, Christmas or Chanukah, egg hunts at Easter and a few others here and there. They're special, but predictable. We love the holidays, the celebration, but we get to know them all too well.

Empty Pages in the Scrapbook

Most families in our culture do too little to recognize this time of life. Few rites of passage mark the many important transitions in our children's lives. Adolescence is one great big time of transition. It's a time when one learns to make important personal decisions, when one moves from being a child to becoming an adult. It's a time when one learns to live as an individual within the community, and it's a time of nascent sexuality. Ultimately, it's a time for a young adult to begin a life separate from their family.

What ceremonies do we have to mark this time? In the Jewish tradition, the Bar or Bat Mitzvah at age thirteen marks the time a child becomes part of the adult religious community. Thousands upon thousands have intoned, "Today, I am a man." Or, as Henny Youngman remarked in recognition of one of the traditional gifts at his Bar Mitzvah at age sixty-nine, "Today, I am a fountain pen."

I became a Bar Mitzvah. I enjoyed the ceremony and the experience very much. My Bar Mitzvah became one of the pillars which supports my Jewishness. However, it took me a good twenty-five years before I fully embraced and committed to the spirituality attached to the ceremony, and by that time, I had forgotten much of what I had learned.

I'm not convinced that this Jewish ritual moved me into the adult community. It certainly marked and celebrated an important time in my life, but it did little to connect me with a continued sense of involvement with my elders. I believe that in both my time and today's world, this ceremony is too separated from the rest of a teenager's existence. The Bar/Bat Mitzvah ceremony is focused primarily on religious tradition and the separation of church and state of mind makes it only partially effective.

Other rites of passage? There are different coming-of-age ceremonies in other traditions. In Mexican culture, the quinciñera is a ceremony for girls who come of age at fifteen. The debutante introduces one's eighteen-year-old daughter to "society," though I'm not sure its original meaning has survived. Informally, coming of age experiences in this culture include the sex talk, getting more freedom from your parents, and getting a driver's license. This last one may be one of the most important transitions. Unfortunately, we don't pay much attention to it, but I'll talk about that later.

We do have high school graduations, which I love. They bring tears to my eyes every time, though I've never felt that graduation ceremonies were deeply meaningful. They mark the end of an era, but without reflecting much on the meaning of the time. None of the pomp and circumstance helps students imbue meaning to their passage through school. Graduations don't provide students with the structure to identify what and how they learned, how they've changed, and what they'll take with them on the next journey.

I may be a bit cynical about what's available to teens in the United States. This is partially because I've listened for years to almost-adults bemoan the fact that they have nothing to do and they feel that nobody really cares. I'm not too far off when I say that little recognition is given for the most potent, touching-the-dark-side, confusing, stretching, seeing-what-else-is-out-there, and learning-through-experience time of our lives. We send our kids from elementary to middle school, from middle to high school, and from high school off to college with little thought, ceremony or ritual to mark the major changes in the experience, physiology and development in our children's lives. Our teenagers need us to be doing something significant to acknowledge this time. Ritual is truly a remarkable teacher, and it seems our culture has a glaring teaching disability.

WHAT DO I BELIEVE?
Part Six

After graduating from high school, my child will:

a. Go straight to college, do not pass go, do not collect $200.

b. If she wants, take a year off before pursuing a college degree.

c. Join the family business. Like the ring of Sanford and Son?

d. Complete a six-month ritual that includes moving out today. Bye now.

I will help my child with post high school work (college applications, jobs, apartment hunting, etc.):

a. Only when asked.

b. Only when asked, unless my child is not doing anything.

c. On all days ending in the letter "y."

d. Rarely, if ever. My parenting days are over.

The Wrong Way to Rite

Almost twenty years ago, I did some graduate work in experiential education. The head of the department was a wonderful man who believed deeply in learning by doing and in learning through metaphor. Ironically, he taught primarily by lecturing and handing out didactic research that supported his beliefs that learning happened best through experience. He also provided us with remarkable learning opportunities. Students taught classes. We participated in adventure education trips to learn new skills. We created internships in the community with people who knew what we wanted to know. And we took field trips, one of which was to the Colorado Outward Bound School (COBS) in Denver, Colorado. Originally created by Kurt Hahn as "the moral equivalent of war," Outward Bound takes groups of people, often teenagers, on trips into the wilderness. In groups and as individuals, these mostly urban kids face challenges which lead to remarkably deep and rapid personal growth. In my private practice, I often recommend these trips for young adults who are very angry, or don't flourish in a talk therapy format. I believe in what Outward Bound stands for.

The director at COBS was a very intense man in his early thirties. He was the jock-outdoorsman-meets-burgeoning-executive type. He led us to the conference room and began to speak at us even before my classmates and I had the chance to settle in our chairs. He told us all about the history of Outward Bound and about the Colorado school, then he started in on the importance of ritual. He said that Outward Bound was similar to a rite of passage known in Africa where boys' penises were smashed between two rocks. Ouch!

The men in the group more or less doubled over in mock pain, and the women sat up straighter in their chairs. "So it's a lot like Outward Bound," Janis asked, "women can't do it?" The men laughed again. Our humorless director did not. He went on to tell us that these same tribes had similar rites of passage for women that were just as painful. As you can imagine, that made us all feel a whole lot better.

The director felt that during adolescence it was necessary to provide a ritual so shocking, so painful, and so steeped in tradition that the individual's survival instinct is awakened for both the self and the tribe. He was a true believer.

I have to say that Outward Bound has mellowed over the last twenty years. New directors have adjusted philosophies. Other than creating the Rite of Passage Award for a student in our class (Janis was awarded a small rubber penis tied between two rocks), we left the field trip in agreement about ritual, but in opposition about methodology.

The Rite Way

Personally, I'm not a hard core, smash-anything-between-anything-else kind of guy. I'm not a ritual piercing or tattooing kind of fellow either. Anything that's going to mark me for a long time, I can do without. Heck, I never believe in anything long enough to put a bumper sticker on my car. Visualizing whirled peas made me laugh several times in the early 1990s, but okay already, move on. Find a new joke.

The type of ritual I like isn't a gigantic deal. When a rite of passage hits the mark, it grounds the participants in the present, teaches about the gifts of our past and makes memories for the future. Any ceremony, when done correctly, bestows importance and meaning on the everyday. It teaches reverence for and appreciation of life in all its twists and turns. It teaches us how to live well.

Though it's nice to celebrate the everyday, I can only imagine your teenager's response should you suggest that the family awaken at 5:15 in order to celebrate the sunrise. "Right Mom, in your dreams I'll give thanks for the new *#@&! day!" (Don't forget about a teenager's sleep patterns)

As always, pick your battles. Only times of change are truly suitable for ceremony. The transitions in our lives provide more opportunity for growth than any other. In the shifting of our psychic weight, we become better able to feel which muscles need to be stretched, and which need to be massaged. Endings are, naturally, a time for reflecting on what worked, what was meaningful, and what begs to be carried into the future. Beginnings are an excellent opportunity for setting your sights above the horizon, for planning for the future, and for taking stock of your skills and gifts. Life's changes are inevitable, but growth is optional. Honoring a moment with reflection and celebration can bring great strength to the next experience. Growth becomes attainable.

Finding a Common Meaning

Let's talk about driver's licenses again. In most states, at age sixteen you can get legal access to the open road. You take driver's training, get a permit, drive fifty hours in the car with one parent discretely clenching her fists, take the test and, whammo, you're a licensed driver. Many adults fail to realize that, for so many teens, a driver's license is the equivalent of a kite soaring off into the wild blue after its tether has been cut. Getting a driver's license means freedom.

Without really being aware of it, teens look forward to the experience as a ritual. One of my clients pulled in and wouldn't do any extra activities for the three months before his sixteenth birthday. There were things this young man wanted to do, but he just didn't want to ask for any more rides from his parents. He didn't want to wait for one more bus as the temperature fell alongside the autumn leaves. He didn't want to be dependent on anyone, friends or parents. Home was a better alternative. Once my client got his license however, he was off and running again.

This young man is like most driving-age teenagers. He obtained a license and was on his own much more often. If your daughter can both procure and drive the family sedan, she's a step closer to full independence. No one has to pick her up. With a driver's license, a teenager is on her own — almost.

On the flip side of the coin, parents see getting a driver's license as a privilege. That is, little Susie has to earn the right to drive. My parents of the client just mentioned worried about the fact that he just sat in his room prior to his sixteenth birthday. Now they're telling him he isn't concentrating enough on school. If he can't maintain focus on school and the future, they'll curtail his driving. Many parents tie a license to good grades and particular behaviors. Often, the parental message is "Do as we say, or you won't get what you want." In the worst of situations, it becomes behavioral blackmail.

I'm not questioning this as correct parental behavior. I'm just pointing out yet another place where parental expectations and understandings don't resonate with those of their teenage children. Getting a driver's license is just one example. They want freedom, we want responsibility. The two beliefs could be connected, of course, but parents too rarely do the ritual work to make it so. This is partly because adults are rarely clear about what they want for their kids, other than that they should be happy. We don't teach them specific skills and beliefs to enhance their independence, so that they will be able to give back to the community. Instead parents hold on for as long as possible, then send their kids off to be independent away from everything and everybody they know.

Walkabout

You might want to see the 1971 movie, *Walkabout*. In it, two young teenagers, with fine English educations, are stranded in a desolate area of the Australian Outback. They are lost and without resources. They have neither the internal or material resources to survive. Without help they will likely die. An Aboriginal boy finds them while on his walkabout. For those of you not hep to aboriginal rites of passage, a walkabout is a six-month solo journey into adulthood commencing about the time of a boy's thirteenth birthday.

A boy who survives his walkabout comes back a man. He is emotionally grounded and solid. He can hunt, cook and take care of himself and others. At the end of the walkabout, his entire village celebrates his return with music, dance, food and love.

If the elders of the tribe fail to prepare a boy for his ritual journey, he might go off into the woods and never come back. One less hunter for the community. One less man capable of fathering children and caring for a family. A great loss. Everything boys of these tribes learn has to be consequential. Lessons taught don't always seem that way to the young, but the adults understand. It is necessary to communicate meaning and insist on compliance. Young people learn everything they need for survival, including lessons about the dark side of the heart and soul. How else could an eighth-grader survive alone for six months with his nightmares creeping about both in his dreams and waking moments?

In the movie, three young people from two very different worlds come together. The young aboriginal male saves the two English children and walks them back to civilization. The movie asks us to consider what will make us capable, self-sufficient and self-actualizing people. In other words, how do we make the events in our own lives more meaningful? How do we create ritual with our own children where there is none?

Making Every Day More Meaningful

Let's use the driver's license for an example, one last time. In order to create meaning and ritual, the first thing parents need to know is the intention of the celebration. Perhaps for the teen, the intention is extended freedom. That is, when she gets her official, get-on-the-road card, she takes another step toward self-determination. In exchange for the freedom and wheels, maybe she has to share in driving of her little brother, or chip in on insurance. It doesn't really matter what the contribution back to the family is, just that the responsibility to her specific "tribe" is clear to all.

Parents should decide what training a teenager needs to be ready to embrace both the freedoms and responsibilities that come with driving. Perhaps a half-hour drive every Monday evening followed by an ice cream cone and a parent-teen talk will help you to know that your little girl isn't quite so little in the driving department anymore. Maybe you want her to be tested out by a less-attached adult friend, to see what he thinks of her driving. Maybe your daughter needs to show you that she can communicate with you about what she's doing on Friday nights.

Next, thoroughly plan your ritual. Who's invited? When is the most appropriate time? Where it will take place? What needs to be done and who is going to do the work? For example, you may want to have a bottle of champagne ready and chilled at the DMV, so that you all can get drunk and drive home together. If you don't like that idea, maybe have a small celebration at home after she's driven around by herself for three hours. Make time for the preparations. If you're using your house, clean before the celebration. The space where your rite takes place is as important and sacred as the ritual's intention and participants.

During your ritual, mark the beginning, middle and end of the ceremony with blessings in whatever form you practice. Personally, I'm not a very religious Jew. I consider myself Jew-ish. I personally wouldn't recite any Hebrew prayers over our family car. But I would take a moment of silence to be grateful for what my family has, for my daughter's gifts and wisdom, and for the safety of my family and others.

Finally, don't isolate your ceremony from your life. If any insight or value comes from your rite, bring that wisdom with you into your lives. Allow your daughter to reflect on and share about responsibility.

Allow her to talk about freedom. Let the others present share their knowledge. Taking wisdom from one experience and using it in another clears the cloud cover from our daily lives. And try to have fun. Enjoy yourselves.

Creating A Ritual That Works

- *Be conscious to mark the beginning, middle and end of the ceremony.*
- *Plan thoroughly and invite important guests.*
- *Prepare the ritual space fully.*
- *Be aware of intentions.*
- *Reflect and share on anything learned.*
- *Attach the ritual to the everyday and follow through with learning.*

Did That. Now What?

Ritual helps to order time and place in a family. Celebrating your teenagers' passage from one stage of life to another allows your kids to notice their growth. They'll become more conscious. Ritual also provides a teen with a place in that great big line my daughter, Zoë, talked about. As Einstein said, "If I can see farther, it is because I stand on the shoulders of giants." Giving your teenagers the wisdom culled from ritual puts them on your shoulders. They'll be able to see farther.

One of the greatest complaints that parents launch at their teenagers is "How many times do I have to tell you ... !?" Parents wonder why teenagers can't remember the day before, let alone their ancestry. Most fledgling adults don't imbue the events of their lives with much sense of meaning or history. Ritual will lead to meaning for your teenager. "Clean your room this instant, young man!" doesn't inspire compliance on a gut-level, survival instinct. Your teenager is probably thinking, "Do any chores *really* need doing?" The house could be a shambles before your son started thinking in terms of the meaning and utility of order. If the garbage didn't get picked up, it would only smell when you walked by it, right?

This thought process can extend to school. While even your son can be badgered into agreeing that an education is important for his future, if you ask him to do his math homework, "What's the point?" may be his question/statement du jour.

I believe teenagers are correct to question some of the expectations placed upon them. Some of us do live conscious, thoughtful existences, but the rest of us have bought into lives that are so full and fast-paced that much of what we do has lost its meaning. We aren't doing what we want or might have chosen for ourselves. We've forgotten the original meaning of our actions. We just do "what has to be done" maintenance. Teenagers, generally speaking, are the ones who speak up and ask "Why?" Sorry, Mom and Dad, "because I said so" is no longer an acceptable reason. Your ways don't hold water without explanation anymore. As your teen makes a life that's his own, he must look carefully at everything that you hand to him. Without meaning, much of what you present will be rejected or resisted.

The Flavor of Meaning

Okay, it's a difficult task to infuse meaning into cleaning the bathroom. But if you give ritual and rite of passage an honest shot, you probably won't have to fight over chores as often. Rite of passage begins when one adds the flavor of meaning to all that happens. Sitting down to eat a meal is an example. Not all families say grace. At dinnertime you might just scream for everyone to come to the table, then you dig in. Nothing gets said about where the food comes from, or what has been done to prepare the meal. No thanks. Nothing. You simply eat.

On the other hand, when I eat a meal with my friend, the Rabbi, we say the Hamotsi, the Hebrew blessing over food. Other friends of mine do something similar when they sit down to eat. I'm always amazed at what I get out of the small act of saying thanks before a meal. When I give thanks, I understand that there's more going on than chewing and swallowing. Somebody, maybe me, took the time and cooked. Someone spent or gave money to provide the food. I recognize something bigger than myself. It helps me to be a little more aware of my enjoyment. In this way, my life takes on greater importance. I even read a study that showed that the body retains a greater percentage of vitamins and minerals from food when grace is practiced. If you prepare your mind and body, you can, literally, reap greater benefits from the food you eat.

The dinner ritual we do practice in my house is a sharing of our best and worst moments of the day. Each person takes a moment to reflect on the day and to share what he or she wants about what was good and bad. The activity involves equal amounts of sharing and listening. It is a sweet time for each of us to be heard. I find that this sharing often leads to much deeper conversations about our lives. Away from the table, my daughter generally responds to questions about her day with grunts and nods. At the table, my family forges the time and space to hear about specific moments in our lives.

Unfortunately, saying grace is usually too pat an answer. Developing a driver's license ritual may make your child only a tad more responsible. But including meaningful ritual can, if nothing else, give your family a sense of history and identity. When I include the larger picture and some of life's mystery in my everyday I find that I have greater awareness and appreciation of what is in front of me. Someday, maybe tomorrow, when you do the same, ritual will provide more depth and meaning for your teen.

International coffees aside, when you celebrate the moments of your life, you begin to act as you envision yourself. You can create a life of grander vision. You act more consciously and, by default, you start eliminating some of your more stupid choices. Rites of passage can bring you a clearer vision of what you want. They'll make your actions more creative. You can leave behind those old patterns of behavior that are like fingernails on the chalkboard of your psyche. You can begin to bring along the patterns that are important to you.

It may be very difficult for your teenager
to speak the whole truth when she's facing
a month in solitary confinement
for drinking she did two weeks ago.

Chapter 7

I Never Exhaled

Corrupted At Last

I've smoked pot twice in my life. I've never done any other drugs, not even one puff on a cigarette. Yes, I drink a little alcohol, but I'll talk about that later. I tried marijuana because a woman I was dating enticed me to join the club. The first time was a Friday night during the summer I was twenty-two. It was at the end of a great date. Julie and I had gone to see *Mrs. Frisby and the Rats of NIMH* at the drive-in. Afterward we walked along a stream, talking. We arrived back at her apartment at 3 a.m. She was smart and, in my opinion, very sexy. She had luscious brown eyes. It was hard for me to take my eyes off them.

She asked if I ever got high. "No," I answered. "Why?"

"Because I want to get you stoned."

I tried to look cool, but I was twitching with excitement and terror. "If I say yes," I replied, my voice trembling, "I need to know why."

Those eyes looked right through me. I would have done anything she told me. "I want to corrupt you!"

I got stoned that night because I thought it would get me laid. That never happened. Both times we smoked, she talked about her ex-boyfriend. Once I stared at the curtains and really got into the colors and the plaid. The second time, I stared at the wall: it must have been fascinating. I quickly discovered that I liked not getting stoned much better than I liked putting something burning into my lungs and not getting laid. It's entirely possible that, had my experience with marijuana and Julie been different, my first-hand knowledge of drugs would be much greater. But the experience stayed as it was, so all my knowledge of drugs is professional, academic and vicarious.

I have this recurring daydream where I make a serious challenge for the presidential nomination. At one press conference, a reporter finally asks about my drug history. In front of the nation, I tell the story. Some supporters and critics are shocked. Some applaud my forthrightness. However, my conviction and honesty win out in the end. It's a great fantasy.

I have no plans to run for President, or Drug Czar for that matter, but when I present to teachers and parents, I tell them about my short excursion into drug usage. I tell the story to teenagers in my private practice if the topic of drugs comes up – and it almost always does. Speaking honestly about my experiences is very helpful in creating an open dialogue about drugs. Being honest about my usage sends a very clear signal to teenagers. It tells them it's okay to be honest. It shows that talking about an issue, even one that's taboo, can help move them to a healthier place.

If your drug usage was more extensive than mine was you might think, "Easy for you to say. If my child really knew how much I used back then, and about the small amount of pot I (might) still do, well, I'd be in serious trouble." Maybe, maybe not. There's no way to know for sure. What I *am* sure of is, if you want your child to have integrity, you'd better practice it yourself. Lies of omission don't work either. They're still not from the truth.

Honesty is better than the alternative, ninety-nine times out of a hundred. As it is now, teens don't usually communicate with adults about drugs. Drugs make up one-third of the triumvirate about which teens rarely talk with their parents (the other pillars being sex and rock and roll). Your adolescent is probably thinking, "If I told you everything, half would freak you out and you wouldn't understand the rest. I don't want to disappoint you, and I don't want to get in trouble."

Even when we don't understand everything that's going on and we freak out a little, we both know that seeing your child fully is much better than the distance created by dishonesty. Painfully though, the relationships we create with our almost-adult children preclude complete honesty about drugs. We don't talk about our own experiences, and, what do you know? They don't talk about theirs.

It's not just parents who create a vacuum in the honest dialogue about drugs. I worked in high schools for more than ten years. Whether or not I agreed with every teacher on educational philosophy, I found most of them interesting and complex with so much life to share. I think of the math teacher who was deeply spiritual, and occasionally read my Tarot cards. The principal with a different cultural experience than mine was a kick in the pants (that's a good thing!). A blues-loving language arts teacher always enthusiastically greeted me with "Where you at?" However, the students at these schools knew little of the lives of their teachers. They were only allowed to see the "grown up, professional side" of their instructors, rarely the whole person.

Needless to say, the kids and their teachers didn't share much. In math, they covered math. Social studies, science and language arts worked the same way. Relationships rarely deepened beyond subject matter. Of course, there were exceptions, but intimacy and opportunities for non-academic growth were mostly lost. This loss was tragic because, along with parents, teachers are the adults who spend the most time with our teenagers. Adolescents learn to have relationships with others through their relationships with parents and teachers. Too often, we hide ourselves from them because we think that if our children really knew us, they would duplicate our imperfections.

Clear Message, Poor Reception

It doesn't work out that way. When we share vulnerabilities, concerns and feelings with our kids, our kids feel closer to us. I count as some of my sweetest memories the few times my parents showed me their passion and grief. My father, who just doesn't like emotional messes, will occasionally share with me something about his past. His sharing dredges up old pain and makes him vulnerable, but it's the information about him that I hold most precious. Knowing some of the "bad stuff" didn't encourage me to repeat his ways. Instead, it's given me insight into *me*. It's helped me love my dad that much more. In addition, the simple act of sharing opens up a pressure valve that is seriously in need of releasing.

I believe our conversations about our drug histories can create a similar effect. The secret is, the sharing of information must be two-way. Your teenage is not going to start the conversation. When you share with your child honestly about who you've been, they can share with you about who they are becoming.

As stated, teens generally don't talk with their parents about drugs. Teens see their behaviors and beliefs as different from what they perceive to be their parents' beliefs. Most teens assume that adults believe that drugs are bad, period. Almost every message we've sent them in this arena tells them it's so. Who can forget the "This is your brain. This is your brain on drugs" campaign. My favorite public service announcement showed a woman spinning around, camera tightly focused on her seemingly euphoric face, with a voiceover telling of her dreams of becoming a ballerina. As the camera angle widens, you see the women in her true state, a drug-induced stupor. A different voiceover intones, "No one ever planned to grow up and be a junky." These are very effective and slick messages.

Parents created these advertisements. At least, parental pressure on politicians created the ad campaigns. The same pressure and mindset created the D.A.R.E. program in schools. The Drug Abuse and Resistance Education program brought police officers into elementary schools to teach kids about the evils of drugs. The strategy was to scare kids by showing how drugs ravaged their minds and bodies. Anything and everything about drugs was bad. Young people were sometimes encouraged to inform the police of anyone they knew who used drugs, including their parents. Several studies have shown this program to be the least effective in reducing substance use and abuse. Still, the message sent was clear.

Parents also give the message directly to their children. "Don't drink. Don't do drugs. They will destroy your mind, body, relationships, opportunities, and future. Life is great. Don't throw it away on a quick fix." Most teens with whom I've worked have also had at least one adult tell them of the many friends whose lives were destroyed by drugs. Everything points to the same message. "Drugs are BAD!"

However, something has gone wrong in the delivery. For some reason, beyond a few minor fluctuations, substance use among teens has remained fairly constant over the last decade. According to a recent American Drug and Alcohol Survey, by their senior year in high school, 82 percent of teens will have imbibed alcohol and half will have smoked marijuana. Roughly one-sixth of all teens (15%) will have used hallucinogenics like LSD. It isn't that our children aren't listening. They can recite statistics and spout the adult company line about drugs en masse. Teenagers understand that, when we implore them to "practice, practice, practice," we aren't talking about substance abuse. Still, the message isn't having its desired effect.

Teens continue to use alcohol and other illegal drugs for two main reasons. First, we (parents and society at large) haven't been honest with our young people about how and what we use. The truth is, we're a culture that deals with physical and emotional discomfort by using all sorts of numbing, instantly gratifying drugs. Even when the drugs are neither numbing nor instantaneous, we still act as though drug-induced change is better than dealing with ourselves. We may tell our young'ns that "drugs are bad," but our behavior suggests that drugs will ease their pain, help them to relax, make them socially more comfortable, put them to sleep, keep them up, and make them more alert. Our actions say, "We use drugs because they work!"

In other words, if you don't feel well, fix it fast. If you don't like the way you look, change it fast. If you don't like the way you are, adjust it fast. Have a headache? Take a couple of Bayer or Anacin or Tylenol or Advil. You'll feel better in twenty minutes or less. Losing your hair? Rogaine to the rescue. Feeling depressed? Don't worry about the stress of your job, problems in your marriage, or alienation from you children, join the McProzac nation — over three million served. Just take the pills and don't worry about the side effects.

At the very least, if you can't fix it, change it or adjust it, simply forget about it. A few belts of this scotch and a couple of cans of that beer should do the trick. In fact, the American Medical Association recently stated that having three drinks every day is considered moderate use. The western medical model is designed to eliminate illness, not promote health. Absence of sickness is the goal, not health and wellness. For example, with my "health insurance" plan, wellness benefits aren't available for the first six months after enrollment. Sickness benefits kick in immediately.

The message is everywhere. Watch television. Read a magazine. Look at the T-shirt over there (No, not the Barney the Dinosaur T-shirt — the one with the alcohol advertisement). You get the message. Drugs work! Maybe you think distinctions must be made between legal and illegal drugs. I agree — taking Tylenol and dropping acid are two very different experiences. However, for the concrete, black-and-white mind of the adolescent, the lines of differentiation are as blurry as those on the street after your third margarita.

Granted, the societal attitude toward substance use is changing, but the medical, insurance and pharmaceutical industries are still geared toward eliminating what ails you as quickly as possible. Legal drugs bring quick remedies and high profit margins. Shoot, I just read in *Newsweek* that the pharmaceutical market for pets is over $3 billion a year and growing. Don't get me wrong. I don't intend to come off as an anti-drug zealot. My forty-year-old knees appreciate their aspirin-like pain reliever after exercise. I've seen very positive effects from drug treatments for mental illness. I am not a teetotaler when it comes to alcohol. I enjoy the buzz. The point here is honesty about use, not abstinence.

Can't We Talk About It?

The message fails to lessen our teenage children's drug usage for another reason. Generally, we send a hard-line message that leaves little room for discussion. Teenagers always want room for discussion. You have to realize, it doesn't matter what your message is. If you don't recognize teenagers' own ways of looking at things (or the "right way," as they see it), the message will be ignored.

Yet we keep sending it, just like we have for the past two decades. I once watched Nancy Reagan advocate this tough love stance on drug use at a White House banquet. She literally raised her glass of wine to "Just Say No." And "Just Say No" is still a very popular strategy for the parents of elementary-aged kids and younger teens. The theory is, kids will turn away from the devil's playthings, because they have a clear boundary behind which to stand.

Some kids may not start to use drugs because of this strategy, but others experience abuse nonetheless. That's why we started the War on Drugs. Zero Tolerance, and go directly to jail. I've never agreed with this methodology. We should start peace talks with all users. Not doing so costs our families, our communities and our pocketbooks. Vilifying users only serves our prison systems.

On the flip side of "Just Say No" is the "Just Say Yes, But With Me" approach. In this strategy, a parent anticipates that her teen will experiment with drugs and alcohol. This parent did his share of mind expansion in the '60s and '70s. He probably still drinks a healthy amount of alcohol when he parties, but he has it under control. In order to make sure that everyone stays cool, he buys the keg and has the party at his house. This way, he can keep an eye on what's happening and guide his child through the turbulent waters.

I know of a number of parents who carry out this strategy. I admit to a twisted sense of relief knowing that seventy-four teenagers are partying with parents in attendance, rather than unsupervised in the mountains. The thought of teens with blood alcohol levels twice the legal limit, driving down a serpentine canyon road, scares me. This relief never stays with me though. I never recommend that you throw the party. Furthermore, this tactic does nothing to address the problems created by the "Just Say No" gambit. It only flips the coin to the other side. Both approaches are extremes, which fail to factor in the full complexity of the issues.

So how does a caring, slightly frightened parent get honest with their kid? Easy. First, take a very good look at what substances you imbibe. Do you smoke? If you do, your children probably will too. Do you drink? I do. I have one to two drinks per week. I'm very conscious of how much and how often I drink in front of my daughter.

Smoke pot? I know of a lot of parents who smoke pot regularly. They still hide their stash from their families. They wait until the little ones are safely in bed and fast asleep. Do a little toot? Acid or 'shrooms? Nah, that was back when you could ride on a roller coaster and not get sick to your stomach. What about a little Ecstasy now and again? One of my clients recently told me that he sold twenty-seven pills of "X" to a neurosurgeon. If this guy has children, watch out. If you use any drugs, your kids will find out. Trust me, I hear about it all the time. If you're trying to hide your use, examine the reasons. Chances are, no matter what you're doing, if you tell your daughter something other than the truth, it'll appear hypocritical.

Second, I suggest that you let your child know what, how much and why (or why not) you use. Take some time to figure out what you learned from using. Re-discover what you've learned from stopping. Don't tell war stories — as much fun as it is to recollect the week you dropped twenty-five hits of kick-ass blotter acid, it won't aid your teen in making wise, informed decisions about their drug use. Aim for the sharing of wisdom.

That's right, you have wisdom. When you talk about your own learning and experience, the student, or in this case your son, can take what is useful for himself. By sharing your knowledge and not focusing (yet) on your kiddo's actions, you own the issue and take responsibility for your behavior. You act the way you hope your kids will. They'll get it. At least, they'll get some of it now, and the rest in their twenties. Then they'll return home to apologize for everything they did to torture you. You'll be setting up honest and respectful communication as the norm in your home. Your child will join in the conversation, maybe a lot.

A Continuum of Use

Here's one way that both you and your teenager can look at and talk about drug usage. Developing a common language with your teenager helps. Take a look at the continuum below and figure out where you all stand (or fall if you're on the "Dependent" end of the continuum). Don't *judge* anyone's use, just find out where you are to start. This continuum applies to illegal drugs, plus alcohol, and the inappropriate use of prescription medication. Leave out cigarettes, Twinkies and coffee. For now.

Alcohol/Drug Use Continuum

No Use | Experimental Use | Regular Use | Abuse | Dependency

"No Use" means exactly what it says. This isn't sipping a bit of the Sabbath wine on Friday evening. I'm not talking about one hit off of your college roommate's twenty-year-old bong when you see her once a year. "No Use" is abstinence.

"Experimental Use" is use to explore drugs' effects. My excursion into the land of weed was definitely "experimental." I never got to a place where I knew how smoking affected me. Was I stoned at the time? Perhaps, but I needed a little more practice to know for sure. If you're honest, you can distinguish between "Experimental Use" and

"Regular Use" easily. It's not "Experimental Use" if you are "experimenting" Monday with pot, Tuesday with LSD, Wednesday with cocaine, Thursday with speed, Friday with booze. That's a very different spot on the continuum indeed.

"Regular Use" is where most normal users (whatever normal is) find themselves on the continuum. A regular user is beyond experimental use. He knows how drugs affect him, body and mind. Generally speaking, a regular user indulges responsibly and without incident. He doesn't light up a doobie at 4:20 every day. He doesn't necessarily drink with his buds every Friday and Saturday night. It has little to do with uniform behavior. It's about experience with a substance.

"Abuse" can be measured in two ways. As we approach the high volume intake end of the spectrum, we're talking about excess. So one way to look at abuse is by determining the amount imbibed. When I drink, for example, I generally have one or two. That's all. I'm not trying to get "faced," but to enjoy the effects of my liquid nervous system depressant. This is how people (that is, people without drinking problems) drink.

Abusive drinkers don't sit down with their friends, talk about the stock market and sip a martini or two. They get blitzed. They want to feel reeeeeally drunk. Bring on the beer bong! Ask any teenager to give you a percentage of her friends who drink to get drunk and the number will be surprisingly close to 90. That's the percentage of teens who drink abusively. Again, don't *judge* the behavior for now, *identify*. Though smoking marijuana is slightly different (both because of the legality and because of the physical consequences), the excess rule still holds. Those who are potheads easily identify the difference between taking a few hits to get high and smoking a few bowls to get baked.

Another factor in abusive use is the consequences of use. From initial experimentation, it's possible to have problems associated with alcohol and other drugs. You might find that your friends or significant others are angry at your behavior. Parents can be furious if they catch their teens under the influence. Use can bring about problems with school or work. All kinds of health problems can spring up. Problems like "Wow, my nose is broken. I wonder how the gutter jumped up and grabbed my face like that," or if one gets sick after a weekend of partying. I know, it was fun until you started staring at the inside of the American Standard.

Legal issues abound. For example, have you ever noticed that you can only get a DUI when you're drinking? Decisions made about sex and sexuality are also problems that arise — no pun intended. I don't have any research to back this up, but anecdotal evidence in both my private practice and in high schools suggests that better than half of all teenagers lose their virginity under the influence. And what about money? Drugs can be expensive. If your teenager is committed to practicing a lot in order to get his abuse down pat, it's going to cost him. A friend of mine who quit drinking admitted to spending close to $500 a month on alcohol. Where does a teenager get the money to supply his crack cocaine habit anyway?

No problem related to substance use, if it only happens once, constitutes abuse. They're what I call "stupid problems" with alcohol or drugs. With stupidity, one can get smart with relatively little effort. If you're paying attention and don't want trouble, you just change your use pattern by cutting back or stopping. Then, you're good to go for not-getting-in-trouble. Abuse is a recurring pattern that cycles from substance use to the occurrence of a related problem, to continued use in the same manner as before, and then back to the creation of more problems. In other words, abuse is drug and/or alcohol stupidity multiplied, then reinforced by the same stupidity.

"Dependency" is the use of alcohol and/or other drugs to maintain some sense of normalcy. It's addiction. This dependence can be physical, emotional or both. It is very difficult to assess whether a teenager is physically addicted to any substance. Certainly, identifiable signs show up in some teenagers.

Physically, addiction is the inability to function without the substance. Withdrawal, though present even when substance use is limited, takes the driver's seat and then does its best to lock you in the car. However, dependence in teens usually takes the form of emotional addiction. For some teens, substance replaces all coping mechanisms.

Instead of learning how to deal with life, aspiring junkies use pot, alcohol, speed, or whatever to address their problems. We know it doesn't work, but that doesn't matter. When use hits this point on the continuum, the user becomes committed to proving us wrong. The battle cry of the addict is denial.

On the other side of the fence is the parent who over-worries about addiction. Teenagers who get into a lot of trouble are not necessarily living with drug dependence. To this parent, a little trouble looks like a mountain of problems. Only when a user can't imagine any option other than further use is she getting close to the dependency point.

Using Your Knowledge for Good, Not Evil

Can you identify where you are on the continuum? It doesn't have to be exactly at one point or another. You can be in between any two use points. What problems have arisen from your use? I have an older teenage client who came to me after a long string of events, the first of which was a non-drug-related arrest. While in the court system, he failed two or three drug tests. It turned out that he'd been stoned at least once every day for the past two and a half years. What didn't initially look like a drug problem, started to smell like serious dependence after a few sessions. This young man was able to be very honest with me about how he used; he simply couldn't see that his drug use had caused most of the problems he was facing.

During heavy drug use the skill you develop most proficiently is rationalization. When you become attached to drug use, it becomes possible to rationalize any behavior. Remember how in fourth grade you would preach to anyone, including your dog, "Drugs are bad! I'm never, ever going to use drugs! I swear." By the end of your sophomore year in high school, you were doing your best stoner drawl and saying, "Dude, pot's not bad. No way, 'cause it's, like, natural. Yeah! It's God's herbage, dude."

Now you've managed to get honest about your current and/or former drug use. You've looked honestly at the problems that have arisen from it. You're clearer about why you used and why you stopped. Here are three more variables of use that will help you focus more clearly among the different use points of the continuum: set, setting and mindset. With set, setting and mindset, you will be better able to place yourself along the continuum.

Set is the *substance* you're using. Teenagers' drugs of choice are still alcohol and marijuana. In the part of the country where I live, acid and mushrooms are next on the hit parade with different forms of speed a close fourth. Although it's not unheard of, teens who use heroin are outside the normal loop. By that point, the user is definitely at the far end of abuse or into dependence on the continuum. Likewise, teen use of prescription drugs (painkillers, for example) is highly abnormal and speaks to dangerous use. For adults, cocaine replaces LSD in the drugs of choice, and prescription medications are up there too, but otherwise, it's fairly consistent. Alcohol, then pot, are the top choices of users of all ages.

Setting is *where* and *with whom* you're using. Are you at a party? Hiding in the bathroom and blowing smoke out the window when it's thirteen degrees below zero? In a car, hot-boxing in the school parking lot? If you do not know what hot-boxing means, ask your teenager. If she claims not to know, ask her friends. Do you use at a barbecue with friends? Some of these are healthy behaviors and some aren't. If you can't figure out which situations are healthy and which are more dangerous, then go directly to abuse. Do not pass go. Do not collect $200.

For teenagers, it's pretty normal to use with friends. Whether you like it or not, it is culturally appropriate and, therefore, regular use. For adults, drinking at a cocktail party or out on the town, likewise, looks normal. An abnormal setting would be your child walking into a crack house or using alone. For an adult, the wrong set would be partying with your teenager's friends. A couple of summers ago, I was walking through the college area of town one evening. I saw and chatted with a few twenty-year-olds with whom I had originally worked with in a high school and whom I had greatly enjoyed. They were on their way to a party. They said I should come along and have a beer with them. "No, thank you," I said gratefully. It wasn't the right setting for me. Understand with whom it's appropriate to imbibe.

Mindset is really important as well. It's the *why* of getting high. In the Jewish culture, drinking is given meaning. You drink to celebrate various holidays and to remember certain events. There's even a holiday when getting appropriately drunk is encouraged. The mindset of the drinker is connected to her Jewishness. In the case of Judaism, one outcome of giving drinking a context is less alcoholism than in almost any other ethnic group.

Unfortunately, teenagers generally don't use for religious purposes. An adolescent's use of peyote is almost never with a shaman-guide to increase his consciousness. Most teenagers just want to get hammered. Teens create all sorts of substance abuse wives' tales to support this mindset. My favorite is that by drinking beer through a straw, you'll get drunk faster.

Few of these tales are scientifically accurate. They just presuppose the "let's get wasted" mindset. And getting wasted is exactly what happens. Back in the '60s, when substance use was really introduced to the general public, the mindset encouraged us to free our minds, love one another, and create a new world of possibilities. By the late '80s, this had morphed into the bumper sticker motto "Reality is just a crutch for those who can't deal with drugs." Still later, the mindset of teens often leaned toward "the world sucks and we should get away any way we can." Though it led to plenty of drug problems, I find the '60s community-oriented mindset more acceptable than the current one, which preaches disconnection.

Getting Clear About What's Enough

Now you really know where you stand. The next step is to get clear on what is too much use for you and your child. This is key. Remember rationalization? Well, if you don't identify the point that's too far on the continuum, you'll rationalize yourself right over the edge. That is, when you're using, it's much easier to convince yourself that a little more of this or that won't cause any harm. Identify this boundary for yourself and for your child before all parent-teen conversations, so you can communicate your values and limits. Please, do the identifying when you're sober. Otherwise, rationalization will rear its ugly head once again.

For some of you, any use will be too much. Others will allow some experimentation. Still other families will decide that regular use is fine, as long as it doesn't get in the way of safety, school and family. Heck, you might find it fine and dandy if your girl goes out on Fridays and comes home completely stoned. I don't have to live with you or your kids, so I don't expect you to have the same limits I have. Find what feels right and try it on. If it doesn't fit, change your mind. Consistency in parenting your teenagers is not about doing the same thing over and over: it's about giving the same message over and over. This is developmentally appropriate. In the case of setting limits with substance use, the message is "I love you and I don't want anything bad to happen to you. I won't allow you to hurt yourself if I can help it. This is what I'm doing about what's happening right now."

WHAT DO I BELIEVE?
Part Seven

When it comes to drinking and drugging:

- a. *Never is too often for my teen.*
- b. *Once in a while is okay, as long as safety is considered.*
- c. *Okay I guess, as long as you never drive under the influence.*
- d. *Dude, pass the roach.*

I want to talk with my teen about their substance usage:

- a. *Regularly.*
- b. *Never, don't they have health class?*
- c. *If I have to. Does it really help?*
- d. *Absolutely, but what do I say about what I did?*

Breaking the Silence Barrier

Now you're ready to engage your child in a conversation about all this. Ask your daughter what she knows about alcohol and drugs, what she thinks she knows, what she's been taught in school, where her limits are and what her friends believe and do. Ask your precocious child to identify where she thinks she is on the continuum. Implore her to be honest.

Now if you're going to ask your child to be completely forthright, you might have to call a cease-fire from consequences for the time being. It'll be difficult for your teenager to speak the whole truth if she's facing a month in solitary confinement as a punishment for drinking at a party two weeks ago. A few years back, I worked with a father and son around this issue. The son really wanted to be "fully himself" with his dad, but he didn't want to be "fully in trouble" either. The dad wanted to know his son, but didn't know how to draw him out.

It took a few sessions of negotiation, but the two agreed to try a two-week period in which the son let his dad know where he was going, what he was going to do, and (after the fact) exactly what had happened. For two weeks, there were no punishments. In return, the father was given assurance that his son wouldn't drive, nor get in a car with a driver who was, under the influence. Moreover, son and dad agreed to converse with each other about what was happening.

After the two weeks, dad decided he didn't want to know everything his teenager was doing. It was simply too much information. When the trial period ended, conversations between the two were fuller, but not over-the-top. The son eventually started using less because getting drunk was less exciting as an above-board activity.

During this exercise, father and son started talking together without shame, anger and punishment. They started to share values about what was happening in the son's life. Remember, the point for parents is to have conversations about values, not to give an impressive forty-five minute lecture to an inattentive teenager.

As you talk with your daughter about her use, make part of the conversation be about the benefits she derives from substance use, legal and illegal. If you can identify what your all-too-experienced teen is trying to obtain through use, you can better help her learn how to cope, enjoy, and learn without drugs.

Furthermore, don't let up until your almost-adult talks with you. Do not let silence or grunting become a substitute for a real dialogue between the two of you. Use electrodes, if you must, to get your child to open up with you. The first shot you take at this conversation may be stiff. Don't give up. The more you're willing to share and to listen, the easier the conversation will become. I believe with all my therapeutic heart that the development of honest and open communication between parent and child is more effective in preventing substance abuse than any public service announcement ever aired on MTV.

Finding Healthy

There are loads of theories about how to save your teenager from the evils of drugs. No single one works absolutely for everyone. You may have to try your hand at several, including the War on Drugs, before you find one that works for your family. Recent research on addiction recovery has shown that it takes numerous interventions before the user embraces real change. The interesting implication is that the first however-many failed interventions aren't failures at all. Each one contributes to the addict's eventual recovery. This may be an extrapolation stretch, but I think it's the same for those not addicted to drugs. When there is a problem, you try some sort of solution. If it doesn't work, you try again ... and again ... and again. When something does work, it's the combination of all your efforts and caring. Don't sell any of your actions short, even the ones that don't seem to immediately work.

Consciousness of your child's and your use significantly decreases the chances for substance problems to develop or continue in your family. It's a lot like becoming healthy in other ways. For example, weight management. The "Just Say No" approach to food has never worked in my life. Dieting and fasting don't address my long-term health issues with eating. After every diet I've tried, I gained back the weight I lost and added a few pounds for good measure.

In my life, with food, what I've done is educate myself around nutrition. You're doing the equivalent with your teen by reading this and other books. Secondly, I now read the labels on the food that I buy and eat. Getting clear on your use and limits, and encouraging your adolescent to do the same, is label-reading of the parenting kind. My awareness and desire to be healthier has led me to make different eating choices. I exercise more, eat better and, consequently, lose weight with much less effort.

The "Just Say No" approach doesn't curb your child's bingeing or develop healthy habits around dealing with stress and drugs. It's a quick fix approach. With drugs and your teen, your awareness and desire will lead you to talk with your not-so-little one about drug use. You'll learn what your child has to say and encourage his voice. If he does use, he won't have the "screw-you-I'm-doing-what-I-want" mindset. By engaging your teen, you will be better able to set solid limits around substance use. Chances are, it will also lead to fewer problems and better health for your teen.

The majority of parents with whom I work start out unaware of what their teens are using. Many are aware of their own use, but stop there. These parents adopt what I call the "Don't Ask, Don't Tell" policy with regard to teenage substance use. They call family press conferences to extol the virtues of a drug-free life. Ask them, and they'll tell you that they worry about their kids, and that they're keeping an eye out. They don't want any drug abusers running around their family. At the same time, these parents rarely ask their kids what's going on when they come home looking and acting differently. When they do ask, a report that everything is okay suffices. Generally, the only time they take action around drug and alcohol use is when informants provide these parental politicians with information on the down low.

As I said before, talk to your kids often. Don't be afraid. When I talk with my teenage clients about drugs, I find that it helps to know a fair amount about the drugs in question. Though there's always something I don't know about or haven't heard of yet, my knowledge allows for a fair amount of slang to bounce around without me asking, "What are you talking about?" — a real conversation stopper with teenagers.

If you know what drugs are around and understand a bit about what goes on with them, you may have the faint appearance of hipness. This appearance may fool your son long enough for him to open up and share. It's a good idea for you to know names, effects and how things are used. I have to warn you though — don't start talking slang and trying to be groovy all of a sudden. There is nothing worse than a forty-something parent busting a move and laying down a groove when it ain't where it's at. Ya down wit dat, yo? Aiiiight. Let's kick it wit' the 411. Represent and give me my props. Peace out.

Learning to survive the really difficult times
is the most important skill
you can master as a parent of a teenager.

Chapter 8

It Could Be Worse

You've Fallen and You Can't Get Up

I know why you picked up this book. Either you're currently struggling with your teenager or you're anticipating struggle in the near future. If you're anything like most of my clients, the struggle is here, now. It leapt out from behind a parked car, grabbed you from behind and throttled you. It's demanding your money, your watch, and scaring you so badly you could easily wet your pants.

This whole adolescent thing caught you by surprise. By reading this book, you're hoping that maybe, just maybe, you can figure some way out. You want to break free from the struggle, throw it to the ground and teach it not to mess with you ever again. For some people, this book will be the right one at the right time, and it will set them free. Others will need this book, plus the perfect therapist. Still other families will have to wait for the planets to align before all is well.

For a number of you, luck will not be on your side for the immediate future. You're in for an experience with your teenager that will test your heart and soul, and there's absolutely nothing you can do about it. I can't tell which of you will experience which adolescence with your teen. But I do know this — whether in a short conflagration or a protracted battle, you must learn how to live with the pain life deals you.

Kay is a mom with sweet, loving eyes that betray the pain she's experiencing with her two children. She came to me to figure out what to do with her family situation. Stephanie, the older child, is a teenager. From what I have been told, she's is a passionate, smart, unbelievably willful child striving for the destruction of this part of her family. Kay's youngest is David. He's quiet, and he's following sister's lead. Both kids want to go live with their out-of-state, but very much in-the-picture dad. They'll stop at almost nothing to reach this goal. I've neither met nor spoken with Dad, but from the stories I have heard ... I want to slap him. He physically abused Kay before the marriage ended. Since she left, ex-hubby has taken Kay back to court every year in an attempt to change the annually disputed custody agreement.

Every year Kay faces a new, venomous fight. Every year she chooses to stay with the kids and do what she believes in her heart to be right. Stephanie and David have learned Dad's credo for fighting: hard, long and dirty — don't stop until your opponent gives up.

To give you a taste of Kay's experience with her children, when the two arrived in the airport after spending the summer with Dad, they ran away from Kay, yelling loudly that she couldn't control them. When Kay reached for her daughter so they could talk, Stephanie screamed that she was being abused and called for an airport security guard. The guard did what was reasonable, telling Stephanie who she could call to report a problem.

It wasn't the first time this had happened to Mom. Before she came back to live with Kay, Stephanie threatened that she would call the authorities. In response, Kay called protective services first, and had them interview her daughter, her son and herself. Absolutely no basis for abuse was identified, so no charges were filed. Even so, the familial pain and damage mounted.

More often than not, Kay came to our sessions accompanied by her boyfriend, the not-quite stepfather, Steven. He's a gentle, loving man who really cares deeply about Kay and her kids. Though Steven has a less enmeshed perspective, he experiences his own pain and struggle. The hostility was tearing the family apart.

The constant fighting was threatening to tear Kay's relationship with Steven limb from limb. Since returning in the fall, Stephanie and David were either bellicose with the boyfriend or, at best, aloof. Neither Stephanie nor David showed any signs of weakening in their quest to make Mom so miserable that she sent them back to live with Dad. When I met with Steven and Kay, we all anticipated short-term hell. I thought it would be difficult for the kids to maintain their anger for a prolonged time once they were away from Dad. I was wrong.

At school, Stephanie talked with a counselor about her misery and possible parental abuse. Dad, too, may have called the school and railed on Kay and the situation here. Kay was trying to make it work with and for her kids and she was failing. Kay didn't know what to do.

Should she give in and send the kids back to their Dad? After all, it's what both Stephanie and David said they want. She wants them to be happy and they're miserable with her. But if she does that, she gives into the kids, and then what lesson so they learn? Plus, the evil ex-husband wins and knows he can win again if he fights long and hard enough. On the other hand, if they stay, it jeopardizes her relationship with Steven. He's reaching the point where he can't take the constant barrage of anger, hatred and lies the children are launching at Kay and, by proximity, at him. Kay feels that her only choices are (1) lose your kids or (2) lose your lover. Anyone want to choose from that menu?

Kay is a good, loving parent. She hasn't done anything heinous to her kids, nor propel them to try to run away so quickly and violently. However, that's not the point of this story. Hatefulness has seeped into this family's water supply. Everyone is paying the price of drinking from the contaminated well. You don't need to know or understand what the hell is happening to this family. You only need to realize that this family is experiencing hell.

WHAT DO I BELIEVE?
Part Eight

When I find out my teenager has gotten in trouble at school, I want to:

- *a. Ground her until she is 37 years old.*
- *b. Ground her for two weeks without phone privileges.*
- *c. Help her to deal with the mess she created.*
- *d. Love her, while getting the name of a good therapist.*

To keep anything bad from happening to my teenager, I will:

- *a. Do what I can to control my child's behavior until they're 64.*
- *b. Love them fully, unless they do something really bad.*
- *c. Love them fully all the time.*
- *d. Next question. I can't control this one.*

I wish I could tell you what happened to Kay, her children and her relationship. If there were a happy ending, it sure would make a nice conclusion to this chapter. I could've related to you how she followed my directions and, now, everything is straightened out. Unfortunately, she stopped working with me. But this is what I told Kay. "It may not seem like much, but take care of yourself. Do what you think is best for you first. Don't be afraid to feel all your feelings with your teenager. Don't worry so much about getting angry or sad or confused with your son and daughter. Share. Heal yourself, and don't act from inside the fear and pain. Try parenting from your heart. Do whatever you must from a place of hope, faith and patience. Love your child in this moment, for that's truly all any of us know. From here you have a chance. From this place, things will probably be all right."

Hell Realm

There is a concept in Buddhism called "hell realm." It speaks to the belief that some peoples' lives are, literally, a living hell. I'm not speaking of the Hell of Christianity, complete with Satan and terrors in the afterlife. It's a hell on earth, reserved for the living. When you lament, "My life has gone to hell," it seems that everything, or close to everything, in your life is painful. It describes what happens to most of us at some time or another. Circumstances become such that we believe we have absolutely no control over what's going on in our world. Events can no longer be explained away by one's actions. In teenage vernacular, life sucks the big one.

The events at Columbine High School in Littleton, Colorado, in April of 1999 were a hell realm experience. Kids of varying degrees of innocence were just living their lives. Families believed all was right and calm in the world. Suddenly, shooting opened up in the school cafeteria and everything changed. That day, fifteen people died. Countless others were badly injured. Another student and a parent of one of the injured later committed suicide.

That horror affected every single student, their family members and all faculty at Columbine High School. Why did it happen? Nothing can adequately explain. Knowing that the shooters were ostracized, that one of the perpetrators was on anti-depressants, and that the school's jocks were given too much power, it doesn't make enough sense. One day these people were doing what they always did. The next day, their lives were shot to hell.

It plays out in a thousand different scenarios. A number of years ago, at a colleague's high school, twenty people died in one school year. Teens and adults died of suicide, automobile accident and illness. Everyone in that school was wondering who would be next. During an eighteen-month period in one of my client's life, three of his relatives passed on, he moved from the place where he grew up to a new city where he had no friends, and then his parents divorced.

Hell realm. You can't imagine anything getting better, and you can't imagine how things could be worse. It doesn't have to be tragic either. I once worked with a seventeen-year-old client who had lost his way. This young man was brilliant, but he could no longer function in school. He dropped out, isolated himself from friends, and refused to get a job. He started stealing. His parents were terribly sad, scared, angry and miserable. He shared all his parents' feelings, plus he became obsessed with death.

Learning to Endure

Why am I telling you this? In the first chapter of this book, I talked about how all those other books about teenagers were rather hopeless and depressing. I suggested that this one would be a wee bit more fun and helpful. Now I'm painting a picture of the hardest of times. I'm telling you this because you need to understand — *sometimes no matter what you do, bad things happen*.

I hold fast to the idea that learning how to survive your times of living hell is the most important skill you can master as a parent of a teenager. No parenting trick you learn, no incantation, nothing will help you to stay as sane as a parent than learning the spiritual, mental and emotional discipline it takes to survive the hard times. Honestly, to a lesser or greater extent than already mentioned here, parenting your teenager will bring you confusion and difficulty such as you've never experienced before. The experience of parenting your teenager will provide you with feelings you can't imagine having. There's absolutely no way around this reality.

I offer more proof. I recently ran into a couple with whom I had worked four or five years ago. They have five children. The oldest four, though blessed with their share of challenges, have good adult relationships with their parents. The youngest one, Kim, the reason I came into contact with this family, is a different story. At the onset of adolescence, Kim started screaming to the world that she was living in an abusive household and she couldn't take it any more. As far as any of the counselors, therapists and psychologists involved could tell, nothing had happened. It didn't matter. She was acting traumatized.

At age sixteen, Kim moved out. Her parents haven't seen her for three and a half years. Kim keeps in touch with her siblings, on the condition that they tell their parents nothing except that she's alive and well. The siblings agreed to the stipulation. Kim's mother and father only know the sketchiest of details. They've been told that Kim is happier than she's ever been. They no longer blame themselves, but every day, they wonder what they could have done differently.

It's critical that you recognize that there are, or will be, times when you have no control over your teenager's life. Your almost-adult will have negative experiences upon which you will have absolutely no influence. You won't be able to prevent some of your child's experiences from occurring. If you're unwilling to see this truth, you'll spend the next three to six years fighting for a jurisdiction over your child's life impossible to control. You'll drive yourself crazy. On the other hand, when you recognize this and surrender, you'll discover that, sometimes, all you need to do is simply bear witness to the pain of life. At these toughest moments, don't stop parenting. In these moments, don't give up on your child or yourself. I promise, the best way to walk through this fire with serenity is to keep breathing, and not bite anybody.

An Act of Faith

Adolescence and the parenting of these remarkable creatures are a holographic experience. Looking at what goes on in your family for these five or seven years means looking at a microcosm of the rest of life. It contains the whole of our existence. Teens learn how to learn. They learn what they love and dislike. There's great joy, incredible adventure, mind-numbing pain, unconquerable spirit. The good, bad and ugly reign supreme during these tumultuous years. There is nothing that can't or won't happen now that can't or won't happen later on.

I see parenting your teenager as a spiritual act that requires strong patience and indomitable faith. Faith is the process of believing and behaving in a way that confirms the existence of something that you don't and can't know empirically. Knowledge is not the point of faith. Belief is. Trust is. God, in all incarnations across religions, is one example of how faith is manifested. We may never know for certain whether or not God exists. However, many of us carry on as though the truth were absolute. Our faith becomes a source of strength and direction.

Teenagers are another example of faith manifested. For your little girl to survive her adolescent years and become a wonderful woman, she needs you, the parent, to believe in her unconditionally. She requires you to hold her goodness in your heart. It's imperative that you see your daughter as everything she is, and everything she's capable of becoming. You must hold this vision of her, this faith, when she is being delightful *and* when you're pondering calling the police on her.

Good times with your teenager are easy to survive. Being healthy is simple when you feel healthy. Not that every person I know is nice when they have little stress, but it's infinitely easier to do something good when no tragedy is befalling you. It's the hard times with your child, whatever their magnitude, that require your faith the most. When little Johnny or little Susie is sniffing glue, or finding out about sex at the age of way-too-early, or yelling at you for never understanding them, these are the moments for faith.

Every day, practice seeing your child's highest potential in your heart and soul. Do this, because adolescent developmental processes bring about identity crises which may make it nearly impossible for your daughter to hold a positive image of herself. If you lose the faith, and if she loses the faith, then the worst really might happen.

The Happy Trap

Remember the International Parenting Credo? "All I want is for you to be happy." It's genetically encoded into our parental beings. It's the battle cry for just about every parent I know. It speaks to this assumption: the point of life is to be happy. Learn whatever, so you can be happy. Do this, so you can find happiness. Don't do that, or you won't be happy. Parents who preach this credo spend the majority of their time attempting to create and maintain happiness for their children and themselves. Their children learn well. They want to be happy too.

Unfortunately, you can't get there from here. You see, that simple statement, "All I want is for you to be happy," is based on a faulty assumption. The assumption is that happiness stands alone, and above all else. The assumption makes a value judgment about growth and learning and, ultimately, causes more than its fair share of heartache.

You can't feel joy without touching the sorrow that accompanies it, nor appreciate elation without knowing its opposite, pain. You can't have one without the other. Most of us comprehend this on some level, but in our guts and our hearts, we have difficulty remembering. Inside, possibly without even being aware of it, we're still scarred by the pain we survived in our childhoods. As good, loving parents, we hope our children won't experience the same heartbreaks. We forget that much of our growth came as a result of our struggles. We haven't resolved our losses and hurts. We say, "All I want is for you to be happy."

By adolescence, your son knows the point of life. More or less independently, little big man begins to search for happiness and avoid its opposite everywhere. With friends, with drugs and alcohol, during school activities, with and/or away from family, through work, you name it. Neither he, nor any other seventeen-year-old adventurer ever finds the happy place though. There are always chores, duty, family and school that bring something other than happiness. Frustration, or unhappiness, chases him farther and farther away from where he started. Not only is he now confused, he's also miserable.

As the parent, you watch closely as your child struggles with who he is. It pains you deeply. Guess what? You're not just experiencing your child's pain. You're also feeling your own. Most likely, in a completely unconscious form, you feel guilty about your child's misery. You feel responsible that he's not happy. In my practice, I often bring Moms to tears simply by saying, "It's not your fault." Parents feel such responsibility. "All I want is for you to be happy." What a weight for a parent to carry around.

In response to the guilt, you try to fix your child's pain. The thought goes, "If I can just do this right, my kid will be happy.

Success!" You try something. Your teenager resists. You try something else. Your angrier teen storms off in a different direction. "Where am I going wrong?" you wonder. "I feel terrible. Let me try again." Your son won't let you right now. He can't. It's his work, to do on his own. You don't remember this and you feel nuts, angry, sad, overwhelmed.

Get Rid of the Guilt

The problem is, making happy for your child is an impossible task. Getting to and remaining in happiness is just not attainable. You have to, in this arena, let go of expectations. This is how you do it: Get a big glass jar, one of those mayonnaise jars, that holds five pounds of sandwich lubricant. I don't know many recipes that would use up that much mayo, but you can figure it out. After cleaning the jar, take a large piece of masking tape and stretch it across the body of the jar. Take a permanent marker, any color, and write on the masking tape in big letters THERAPY JAR. Then, any time you feel guilty about how your child is feeling, or think to yourself "I just became my mother," or don't know what to do, or you just want to do something nice for your child, put a dollar in the jar. When your teenager turns twenty-one, give him the jar and say, "Here. I'm sorry I messed up. I was really doing the best I knew how. I still am. Go get a therapist, or a new car."

Get rid of the guilt. Judging yourself and your ability as a parent serves you not at all. It serves your child even less. It teaches them nothing about what to do now, and loads them with guilt later in life. It's not what you want for them or yourself. It will be easier to recognize that happy is not the goal. Then, the hard times, the hell times, can be seen for what they are: as equally important and valuable as the happy times.

I took my daughter and three of her friends to the amusement park last summer. This time the kids were all tall and brave enough to ride all the roller coasters in the park. I got to ride, too. I found that the anticipation of any roller coaster is far scarier than the ride itself. None of the coasters last more than a couple of minutes, but you have to wait in a line for up to an hour before the thrill.

Surviving the Hard Times

- ***Keep the Faith*** *— Believe in your child always. You may have to practice in order to believe, but it's worth it.*
- ***Stop Trying to Make Your Teen Happy*** *— Work on helping your child realize that there's growth and learning in every moment. Try teaching gratitude instead.*
- ***Get Rid of the Guilt*** *— Don't take responsibility for everything that goes wrong. Do the best you can and help your teen do the same.*
- ***Look at the Big Picture*** *— The hard times are not the point. They're part of something on a grander scale.*
- ***Keep Breathing*** *— Teach your teen how to take great care of herself by taking excellent care of yourself!*

Standing in the lines, I watched my daughter and her friends deal with their fear. They talked about it. They threatened to get out of line and wait for everyone else to ride. Their fear made them quiet. I paid attention to my own anxiety. There were a couple of coasters I had never ridden before. In these lines, my heart pounded in my chest. I silently worked at convincing myself that I would have a blast, still I was scared. I had read something about being present even in the worst of times, so I concentrated on breathing deeply — in through the nose, out through the mouth. I was determined to be as relaxed as possible in my fear.

I laughed more on the rides that day than I ever have before, even more than when I was a kid. I was frightened — I couldn't avoid that. Yet my work at calming myself, of taking care of myself, allowed me the full range of the experience. I was afraid, but also elated. Roller coasters are just rides, but they simulate the rest of life. Learning to deal with your fears in one arena will help you to deal with your fears everywhere else. No matter where you go, there you are. My best friend Rick said something that I think was important. He said that if we don't see life as a metaphor, it's going to be a very bumpy ride. He sees all the events of our lives as being broadly analogous to something else. The something else is the big picture. He believes that the signposts of our lives correspond to the spiritual meaning of our lives. Rarely, if ever, is an event about the event itself. No episode is, in itself, the point, but instead it's part of a larger picture, a larger meaning.

Rick wasn't suggesting that we look at everything as an illusion. However, to see events as part of something bigger, something more meaningful which we can't fully comprehend, is very helpful indeed. This means that when your fourteen-year-old sneaks out of the house at midnight, the event does not just signify that he hates the whole world. His clandestine escapade has a bigger meaning. There's a larger picture. You and I may never know what the whole picture looks like, but I promise it's not just about your guilt and pain, or your child's unhappiness.

What Does It All Mean?

At some point in our lives, we all start wondering about the meaning of suffering in the world. Something will happen to us or around us that will make us wonder "Why?" Why is this happening to me? Why did this happen to someone else? Why does anyone have to suffer? What's the point? These are all good questions.

Perhaps suffering takes place so that we might better understand its opposite. We humans rarely learn to give to and love others without experiencing pain and suffering in our own lives. Maybe we need the pain in order to understand how to be happy and live well. Perhaps suffering reminds us to take care of one another and ourselves at all times. In an old Jeff Bridges picture, *Starman*, his character says, "You humans are always at your best when things are at their worst." Pain and suffering could be one hell of an excuse to create beauty and love in the world. I don't know. If you have a more hopeful idea, let me know. I'm open to a better answer.

Honestly, there are going to be times when neither you nor anyone else can stop the pain from coming. Sometimes, the bumper sticker is correct. *Crap happens*. At some point in your life with your adolescent child, no matter what your intentions or your parenting skill, you won't be able to lessen the suffering that accompanies life. At those times, do what you think best. In those moments, have faith that you, your kiddo and your family will survive whatever drags you down. Use the hard times to grow as a person, to love another, to provide others around you with beauty. Isn't that at least part of how you want your child to be?

We spend so much of our lives trying to avoid pain. I talked about this some around the issue of drugs. I know of only a few parents who consciously inflict pain on their kids. Most of us are attempting to create the opposite experience in our children's lives. But we carry the scars of incest, abuse, divorce, alcoholism, other addictions and poverty. Some of our hurts are smaller, but nonetheless painful. We might be confused by losses in our life, by neglect, or by our own parents' over-involvement. Few of us have completely ridden our souls of those old hurts. Now we're doing our damnedest to keep our kids from experiencing the same pain.

It's a wonderful quest, but we're rarely successful at shielding our kinfolk. No matter how hard we try, family garbage does not get healed through our children. It only gets healed in our generation. Family trauma gets passed to our children in a remarkably magical, yet fairly simple manner. If you try to spare your child pain by changing their actions and feelings, your offspring will do one of two things. He can swing the adolescent pendulum clear across the continuum and suffer from the exact opposite problem. For example, a child of an alcoholic will become a teetotaler, become hyperstrict with his own children and demand no use at all. His rebelling teenager will drink wildly and develop a drug or alcohol problem. Talk to a drug counselor about how common it is for an addiction to skip a generation.

The second option is that the child will face the same problem all over again. Say your father abused you. None of the therapists I know would be surprised if you married a man who abuses you and/or the kids. I know, he seemed different. But on it goes. As a mentor of mine would say, it's just the intergenerational transmission of trauma.

Breathe ... In and Out

You want your children to have no pain. I can't help you. Nobody can, no matter what they say. You want your children to avoid horrible traumas in their lives. I understand. I want that for my child also. However, we can't control anyone beside ourselves, so I can't guarantee that one either. We waste countless hours, days and years trying to avoid what we can't escape. The fear, mostly unconscious, haunts us.

Stop trying to avoid pain. My dear friend, Scott, told me he thinks we're supposed to experience pain. Now there's an interesting concept. Instead of trying to avoid it, deal with it. Look back into your life and deal with your pain. Feel it, for goodness sake. Feel it for the sake of goodness. We can't avoid fear, pain, loss, and the hurt that goes with living. We can only avoid suffering the effects of our fear.

My client, Kay, was afraid. She was afraid that she would make the wrong decision. She was afraid for her children's well being. She was afraid of her teenage child's ability to destroy her family. She was afraid of her teenager's self-destruction. Kay was trying to figure out what to do from a place of fear, and every solution looked and felt like more fear. It seemed that there was no way out. Feeling trapped is suffering the effects of your fear.

Another of my clients came to a recent session feeling very good about her parenting. Sylvia pronounced success at carrying out a suggestion I had made to her some time ago. Sylvia has four children who have all been challenging. One deals with drug addiction. Another has a severe anger problem. Still another is barely making it through high school. The fourth is just fine, thank you — so far. In addition, Sylvia gets little support from her husband.

One of the large issues for Sylvia, in addition to the problems du jour, is that she tries to be responsible for everything that happens in her family. When she first started seeing me, she felt that everything that went wrong in her marriage or with her children's lives was her fault. She used to spend every waking minute (and quite a few during sleep) worrying about her kids. The kids resented it, and she was exhausted.

In our sessions, I work with her to let go of her kids. I don't want her to stop caring. That is, after all, the grandest part of Sylvia's parenting. All four children know they're very loved. We work on having the kids and the father be responsible for the messes they create. The family pattern of blaming Sylvia for everything that goes wrong was established long ago. Even if she were nowhere near the craziness as problems arose, her kids would blame whoever caught them — the police, school, friends. Her husband didn't help because Sylvia was always front and center cleaning up the mess. It took a while, but for the most part, she has stopped rescuing her kids from their own struggles. When something goes wrong now, she continues to love her children, offers advice and helps when asked, but she really allows them the experience of self-determination and self-responsibility.

Life has improved for this mother and her family. Sylvia is finding the kind of life she wants to live and is going after it. She includes her kids whenever possible. Sometimes they accept her invitations and sometimes they don't. They still struggle with pot, anger, school and life. But she feels proud of their independent struggles toward adulthood. And she feels proud of the way in which she continues to love her family, no matter what occurs.

Sometimes, I tell Sylvia, things don't go the way we plan. At those times, the most you can do is to clearly, cleanly and strongly love your child. That's it. Always love your child. And Sylvia does it well. She is proud of the fact that, along with whatever else is happening, she manages to keep loving her sons. She feels better and more hopeful. That helps her kids through many hard times. Her love during hard times has actually helped her children resolve the messy situations in which they find themselves.

Maybe you're thinking that you always love your teen. Maybe I'm talking to someone else. But most parents don't love their teens all the time. At some point, most parents start to worry that their child is a sociopath, destined for prison or misery. Most parents get frightened for or of their adolescent and want to run screaming from the room. It's easy to love your almost-adult when she's sweet. The key to parenting a teenager well is to not take it personally when she's a terror. It's critical that you don't over generalize when she's done the same thing wrong for the thirteenth time. At these times, it's important, for your sanity and hers, that you love her well. No matter what. It's as simple as that.

The object of the Parenting your Teenager Game
is to break patterns.
Be creative.
Find new ways of doing everything.

Chapter 9

Here's an Idea

Think for Yourself

When I was in graduate school, my favorite professor, Jules Mondschein, insisted that his students think for themselves for the first half of the semester. After week nine, we could borrow other's wisdom. At the beginning of class, we were on our own. This may sound ridiculous, but hear me out. There I was, in a professional graduate school, learning to be professional. Any of you with an advanced degree will remember how many books you were required to devour to get a master's degree or Ph.D.

In every other class I attended, teachers had me read hundreds upon thousands of pages written by earnest and somber social workers whose writings were possibly the authoritative source about whatever the heck it meant to be a social worker. I learned from my books about the history of social work. I learned about social work ethics. I read lots about client self-determination, statistics in social work, and every other topic I can't remember at the moment.

My fellow grad students and I were regularly required to write lengthy papers using these same textbooks as source material. If any of us had anything to say, we were required to credit someone else as being the source of our inspiration. Our thoughts were always to be based upon someone else's. Our beliefs were to be founded in empirical knowledge. You've been in school — you know the drill.

Jules took a different tack. Like I said, it was a prerequisite for us to think for ourselves in his classes. He required, he prodded, he pushed, he encouraged every single student to speak his or her own mind. He refused to have us read someone else's thoughts until we had created a few of our own. Dear, sweet Jules would barely even tell us what he thought of the topics we were discussing. He didn't even want our minds to be made up of *his* mind.

One of his strongest convictions was that, if you are going to meddle in other people's business, you'd better know what you believe and why. Jules felt, and I concur, if you don't understand why you're doing something in your own heart and mind, you're not going to do a bit of good for anyone else. Anyone's thoughts and beliefs can sound great. If you don't believe in what you're doing, you'll cause a fair amount of trouble for all concerned. I loved his classes. There we were, twenty or thirty social work students, without the help of experts, trying to understand what we were doing. It was confusing at times, but I learned more from Jules forcing me to be the expert than I did in almost any other class I took.

The Secret of Your Success

Let it be the same for you, the parent. You be the expert. Become ever so sure about what you believe and want for your child, before some other know-it-all tells you what to do. So here you are reading a book about parenting. You've been confused, or are anticipating being confused, about parenting this child who is now a sometimes-hostile alien life form in your household. You picked up this book looking for steps A through ZZZ which will allow you to resolve your struggles.

And you've made it through most of my thoughts about surviving your child's adolescence without being handed a prescription for dealing with him.

The secret to surviving your child's adolescence is not in any of the ideas that will follow. I hope that many of them work for you and your family. Many will help. It's just very hard to know which ones will be successful from where I sit typing right now. As clairvoyant or as insightful as you credit me with being, I don't know what your specific values, styles and preferences are and, therefore, I can't create the perfect prescription for parenting in your household. Sorry to say, no shortcut to good parenting is available. There's no way around the struggles that you'll experience with your teenager. There's no way over or under the problems. There's no magic potion that will help you more clearly illuminate the path. The only way to survive adolescence is to go through it, with your eyes and heart wide open.

A few years back, I ran court ordered therapy groups for domestic violence perpetrators and other violent offenders. Every Thursday night for nine months, men who had beaten up their wives, girlfriends or somebody else had to give me $25, then talk about their feelings with fourteen others there for the same reason. Doesn't *that* sound like fun? One time, one client asked another what he would do differently after being arrested, convicted and ordered to treatment. He responded coldly, "I would've stuck him in the ear with an ice pick." A dozen-plus other violent offenders were frightened and held their breaths. The only sound was that of air being sucked out of the room. This client's weapon of choice became his nickname. And you think your teenager can get angry.

Pick a Pattern, Any Pattern

I taught these men, Ice Pick included, information and skills which truly did help them to stop acting out violently towards others. One piece of information that I hijacked and adjusted for working with families of teens is the Cycle of Violence model. The cycle speaks to the insidious pattern of behavior that occurs within almost all violent relationships.

The Cycle of Violence works this way: First, somebody hurts somebody else. Next, the perpetrator feels remorse about his actions. He didn't mean to hurt her. Really, he just couldn't control his anger. Or he didn't see it coming. A honeymoon period ensues. The offender says that it won't happen again. The victim believes him. Flowers and chocolate are given as evidence of change and caring. Everyone walks on eggshells for a while. Then life returns to normal. You see, it's too hard to maintain the honeymoon when tension once again builds where tension has been built in the past. Money problems. Pet peeves. Feelings of rejection. Each family has its own version of unresolved pain that creates tension. Eventually, the perpetrator gets really angry again, and guess what? The violence explodes once more and the cycle repeats itself.

With parents and teenagers, the cycle doesn't necessarily begin and end in violence, at least not the physical sort. Parents and their teenagers get into predictable, non-creative behavior patterns around any and everything. For parents and teens, I call it The Cycle of Frustration. One family I worked with did the same thing over and over again around their teenage son's use of cigarettes.

Tyler's parents didn't want him to smoke. He claimed that he wanted to quit, but never worked on the process. His parents would nag. Tyler would resist. His parents would bribe. He would negotiate a larger bribe. His parents would feel uncomfortable with what they were giving to their son, so they would give with a touch of resentment. He would take their bribe and keep smoking. His parents would find out. Tyler would admit to smoking, but say that he wanted to quit. His parents would nag. He would resist. His parents would bribe.

Round and round it went. The cycle of frustration was perpetrated as every player in the game reenacted old patterns of behavior. With a thousand different families, these unhealthy cycles will play out in a thousand different ways, around curfew, with chores, or about school. Patterns, patterns, patterns.

Breaking the Patterns

- *Identify the triggers that set you off in your relationship with your child. Figure out your "canker sores"— those painful places you bite when you interact with your teen.*
- *Identify your pattern responses once you see the triggers.*
- *Create a list of three different responses for each trigger. Reasonable is best, but the key is different.*
- *Try something different next time. If it works, do it again. If it doesn't work, try something else.*
- *Breathe the whole time!*

Letting the Air Out of the Cycle

The founder of Re-evaluation Counseling, Harvey Jackins, developed a model of how problems develop into uncreative patterns of behavior. Mr. Jackins theorizes that every person, at her center, is zestful, curious, loving — a positive human being. I like that thought.

Jackins believes that hurts and mistreatments happen to all of us. We humans, he contends, are equipped with natural tools to rid ourselves of the pain. We cry, laugh, yawn, shake and talk to release the emotion and heal ourselves. If we're unable to release all of our emotion, then our core is covered up and we respond to the next hurt with a patterned response. That is, we re-act in some familiar way, which may or may not have worked for us in the past. As we repeat the pattern behavior, we feel the same old pain, in addition to the new hurt and/or mistreatment. All of this gets in our way of being who we are — loving, curious, zestful. The old hurts and mistreatments seal off our core and create cyclical patterns of distress in our lives.

Jackins contends that if we're allowed (or allow ourselves) to feel our feelings completely, we can find our way back to our core. The way it works according to Re-evaluation Counseling is (a) A hurt or mistreatment happens to you. For example, a co-worker unthinkingly makes a comment in front of others about how heavy you look. Other people laugh. Your initial response may be to mope and be by yourself. (b) You give yourself the opportunity to feel the sadness and isolation fully, perhaps through tears and shaking. You have a good, cleansing cry. (c) You feel better about yourself, and the next time the insensitive baboon tries to make fun, you find a creative way to say, "Knock it off!"

My daughter often does this before bedtime. She has the ability and space to cry and yell about whatever is in her heart and mind. For the short amount of time leading up to and during her cry, Zoë is in her feelings and pretty vulnerable. But after she lets it out, without us trying to fix or heal the feelings, she's better able to deal with all the complexities of her life. Personally, I'm impressed by her presence and creativity in the face of her day-to-day existence. When I grow up, I want to be just like her. The idea is, when something difficult or painful occurs, from our center, we can create the right response for the specific situation. We can be creative. We can create the lives we want.

Parenting your teenager brings up a lot of feelings. When your child yells at you, or is depressed, or you're worried about her schoolwork, it's painful for you. In addition, your teen's experience will bring up all the old, unresolved feelings from your adolescence, family and childhood. If you don't focus on creativity in your responses, there's not a chance on earth that you won't start acting out a cycle of frustration. Then your kid doesn't have a chance to be creative either.

For our purposes, don't focus so much on Jackins' suggestion to feel all your feelings, though it's a great idea. In my opinion, what's more important is to know that cycles of behavior exist, and to understand how they are created. I would say that most parents of teenagers grind and claw their way into very predictable patterns of behaviors. And kids do the same with their parents. We push the same buttons over and over again. We play out the same unresolved scenarios. We run full-steam into the same brick walls, head first.

Creativity Is the Answer

The object of the parenting your teenager game is to break patterns. Be creative. Find new ways of doing everything. It's what your child is doing in her life — she's trying on new behaviors. Your finding new ways of doing life fits her developmental framework. Your creativity will give you a better chance of finding something that works. Remember, consistency with teenagers isn't doing the same thing over and over again. It's providing the same loving message over and over again, through whatever action works well for you.

There's a fun movie, *The Zero Effect* about a modern day Sherlock Holmes, Darryl Zero. Zero says, about the art of finding something, that there are innumerable things in the world. When you're looking for just one thing, it becomes the proverbial needle in the haystack, and you most likely won't find it. However, if you look for anything at all, chances are that you'll find something of value. Zero suggests that by keeping an eye out for anything, one improves the chances for success at finding something.

Parenting your teenager is just like this. If you're looking for the single, correct parenting move that will fix everything, forget it. If you try lots of things, something will probably work. If you don't, you'll experience insanity the AA way — you'll be doing the same thing over and over again, expecting different results. This is the Cycle of Frustration. Let's agree on this — unhealthy patterns of behavior are insane. They are not now, nor ultimately, productive for your family.

Many parents look for the single, exact correct behavior/ consequence for their teen which will turn the kid around and lead him down the path to academic, social, athletic, relational and familial success. Many parents keep doing their parenting-thing in the exact manner which, up until now, has been so remarkably unsuccessful. In fact, the parenting choices have been so ineffectual and unproductive that the many parents find themselves in the parenting section of their local bookstore in search of answers.

I say, try something new. Be creative all the time. If something works, hail to the victory. If an idea flops, flush it like those goldfish that taught your son about death when he was in preschool. The best concrete idea I can give you is to take care of your heart and soul, always. The greatest gift you can give your teenager is to live a creative, courageous life.

Now, one more time. The first element in raising a healthy teenager (and remaining sane in the process) is to understand how your teenager ticks. The way your teenager acts isn't personal. It's not your fault. It's important to comprehend and appreciate (if possible) the relentless drive of your baby-no-more toward independence. It's going to happen at some point.

There's little you can do to stem this hormonal, adolescent tide. Second, deal with *your* childhood. Disconnect your emotional work from your teenager's. This whole adolescent thing is going to bring up a truckload. Feel it. Think about what *you* need. Watch out for patterns.

Most likely, the adolescent tide will hit your child around fourteen and continue through age seventeen. What happens at ages twelve and thirteen is more analogous to pregnancy than to parenting, in terms of adolescence. In pregnancy, you get a taste of parenting. For example, you'll have to get up in the middle of the night to empty your bladder. However, it's not the same thing as hearing your child cry or waiting up for his return. At twelve and thirteen, you get a taste of adolescence. Your daughter will probably slam a door or two. She's just not at the point of breaking down the door yet. That happens later. At eighteen and beyond, everyone begins to recover and live their own lives again.

Know that it's coming and help your child through it. Don't try to hold them back from their journey. *Parent from your heart, not from your fear*. Try to love your child always. It's nearly impossible to make good parenting choices when you're afraid for or of your almost-adult. Things may go wrong, but probability suggests that your kid is going to be all right. Try to believe it. As one of my teen clients says, "Yo, it's all good!"

Now, finally, to some suggestions.

Dealing with Money

One of the defining issues with teenagers in our culture is materialism. Overall, teens want and have more than we did. I don't think this is generational amnesia either. Objects are very important to teens. So, what can you do to teach your adolescent the value of a dollar? One of the best ideas I've seen comes from the author/columnist/psychologist John Rosemond. Figure out how much you spend on your adolescent child each month. This figure can include food for lunches, dinner, recreation activities, movies and gas in the car (if you pay for their driving). If you want to include clothes, car expenses and other costs, go right ahead. If you want to figure in fewer perks, do that. Next, open up a joint checking account with your child's name right alongside yours. On the first of each month, deposit into the account the amount of money that will cover whatever expenses you want to include.

Dr. Rosemond suggests, in what feels like a punitive style to me, that you only deposit 75 percent of what you figure you spend on your kid. I am not sure why. Maybe it builds character to have to make tough decisions, or something like that. I personally don't think you need to teach your child about poverty right now. They'll learn soon enough about living on Ramen noodles and red beans during college.

Anyway, with money deposited and checkbook in hand, your teen is now ready and able to budget and spend his money any which way he chooses. It's no longer your problem. If for some strange reason, your kiddo bounces a check, don't despair. Pay for the overdraft out of next month's deposit. Your teen will learn soon enough that money is not in endless supply. It might be very difficult for you or your spouse to resist slipping the apple of your eye an extra twenty now and then, but do try to control yourself. Birthdays and holidays can bring a bonus. Day-to-day brings monetary learning.

Cars, Commitment and Insurance

You've heard me rant on about driver's licenses. Driving is a very big step toward independence for teenagers. Still, the question remains, how do you get your fifteen- or sixteen-year-old to embrace the responsibility of driving? The cost of running a car is great. Gas, insurance, repairs, and the costs of purchasing a car add up to a pretty penny. Your family income will help determine some of the guidelines.

Some teens will simply have to save up for a car and insurance in order to be able to drive. Other teens will need to come up with the insurance premiums so that they can cruise the neighborhood in the family's station wagon. Still other families will be able to pay for all of their teen's car expenses.

The principal at my daughter's elementary school gave me a great idea for dealing with all the automotive stuff. What Rick did with his teenage daughter was this: He and his wife were able and willing to buy a car for their teenager. It wasn't anything fancy, just utilitarian transportation. They were also willing to pay for insurance. However, before his teenage daughter could use the car, she had to come up with $500 to put in a Certificate of Deposit at their bank. This money matched the amount of the deductible on her insurance policy. If she damaged the car in an accident, she already had the money to cover out-of-pocket expenses. If an accident did occur, she was also required to reimburse the account back up to $500. If, by some combination of skill and luck, she didn't have an accident by the time she purchased her own insurance policy, then the CD, plus interest, rolled back into her pocket.

Rick required his daughter to think ahead about the full range of possibilities that come with driving. Safety became smart, both physically and financially. Rick's daughter was also expected to contribute monetarily toward her motoring. She wasn't allowed a free ride with her own horseless carriage. If you follow this prescription, it'll take some forethought on your teen's part to ride in her own wheels. Your child will learn about saving. This idea would make even me think twice about doing something stupid in my car. Be a safe driver and earn cash prizes. What a deal!

Another suggestion for dealing with money and driving also deals with insurance premiums. One parent with whom I work gave his teenage driver this incentive: If his child's grade point average was above a 3.0 (B average), then the father was willing to pay for all insurance premiums. The insurance company's discount for good student drivers kicked in at that level, and Dad said he was willing to reward his son for the rest. If his son's grades dipped below 3.0, then the entire premium expense transferred to the student. Dad was not tying in use of the car to grades, just the cost of using the car.

Cars and Grades

Thinking of making a connection between actual use of the car and your teen's grades? Don't do it! There's really no logical connection between the two. I know, I've heard all the arguments. You're trying to teach responsibility to your teenager. Take responsibility for your job (school) and you learn responsibility with the car. The association is hazy at best.

I believe the attempt at affiliating driving and studenting is a thinly veiled attempt to control your teenager. I've never seen this method work. First of all, parents with teenagers doing well in school never use this gambit. It's only the parents of kids who are doing badly in school who try to make this linkage. Second, a youngster can be responsible with a car and ridiculous in school, or vice-versa. Don't tie in grades and the use of the car. This is what I call an anti-suggestion.

Yelling and Screaming

I've worked with a multitude of parents who are very near the end of their rope because of all the yelling and screaming their angry teenagers direct toward them. The teenager/parenting gig is painful and confusing enough. Parents don't need their children and/or stepchildren to be mean on top of the other craziness. Phrases like "Teenagers: Can't live with 'em, go to jail if you kill 'em" are right on the tip of these folks' tongues. Screaming and yelling teenagers are a phenomenon that many families have experienced. It's difficult to maintain a strong sense of love for your teen when so much anger, distrust, disrespect and struggle is being directed toward you, the parent.

When someone other than my child treats me badly, I have had a relatively easy time responding. With a friend, eventually, I'll say, "I'm mad as hell and I'm not going to take it any more. Change or stay away!" With my wife, I might scream back at an even higher pitch, or get help from a therapist. At the very least, most of us can imagine taking care of ourselves in these situations. With a child however, it's not nearly as easy to interrupt the abusive behavior by taking care of yourself. It's difficult to say "See you later" to your son or daughter. You are now and will forever be family. Your son or daughter will always be your baby, and you'll always be your child's parent.

Our responses to our teenager's anger often dwell on the extremes of the parenting continuum. Some parents withdraw in the face of a child's aggression. Instead of dealing with our child's wrath, a parent might allow their teenager to do whatever he wants. To some, no conflict is better than any conflict. The problem with this strategy is that it gives teenagers most of the control. The teen does what he pleases and the parents, rightfully, resent his arrogance and general lack of appreciation. These feelings then cycle into the relationship causing more problems and power struggles. Teens don't feel cared for or valued. They abuse their control, and the relationship gets worse.

At the other end of the continuum, parents expect and demand change. "My way or the highway!" In these cases, don't be surprised if the response from your teenager is more confrontational. Your child is already angry. In her view, you don't understand her. When she becomes oppositional, any hard-line position will likely make her more furious. Though many people believe we won the Cold War with strength, we eventually recognized that the threat of the nuclear arms race only worked for so long. The price was too large if the threat of mutual destruction failed. At some point, we had to stop threatening others with annihilation, cease building weapons and ban testing them. Parenting is similar. Eventually, you have to stop the bombs. Otherwise, the relationship with your teenager becomes nothing more than control through intimidation. Loan sharks and their leg breakers never make very good parents. If this is your style, shift it now, or trust will be severely damaged.

On either end of the continuum, when our interactions are going badly, we're left with confusion, feelings of powerlessness and hopelessness. These feelings easily evolve into resentment and more anger. I've seen this cycle too many times, with too many families.

Angry parents treat their teenage child with the same disrespect and ugliness they received from him. Then the teen takes his turn. And on it goes.

Here's a simple four-step approach to deal with your child's anger. The first step is recognition. Get it into your head and heart that your child will get angry with you. I guarantee this to be true, or your money back. I was angry with my parents. You were angry with your parents. In fact, every human being who has graced our third rock from the sun was angry with their parents at one time or another. It's also written into the prophecies that all future generations will follow suit. It's best to recognize this truth now and not be surprised later when your kid loses his cool with you for the first time.

Four Keys for Dealing With Your Teen's Anger

- *Recognize that anger is on its way … if not now, soon.*
- *Let your teens know that it's okay to be angry, to a point.*
- *Set limits as to how far your teen's anger can go. When the waters are calm, let everyone know the limits.*
- *Reinforce your limits with cement, and rope them off as sacred. If crossed, don't get into a fight. Get out of the way. Deal with consequences later.*

My cousin Barbara recognized this to be true. In preparation for and in response to this anger, Barbara took step two of the four-step plan. She instructed her two teenagers how to deal with their anger. Barbara let Andy and Becky know that she understood that they were going to be angry with her for a variety of reasons. She conveyed that it would be okay for them to rant and rave in her presence. Step three came next. Limits.

Barbara made sure her children were aware that there was a line that could not and would not be crossed. In fact, my cousin let her kids know that they shouldn't even consider crossing the line. For Barbara, the line was "Be as angry as you want toward me, but never call me names or curse at me to my face. If you want to say f#%* you or call me a b*#%@, leave the house or go to your room, close the door, and scream it into your pillow." She may not have been happy with their rage, but she expected and could live with it.

Finally, take the fourth step. Do whatever it takes to make sure your kids understand and follow step three. The way you take step four is to draw the line clearly in the dirt, dig a small trench along the line, mix up a batch of concrete, pour it into the trench, let it dry, and paint it a fluorescent green. Make sure everyone knows without a doubt that you're serious about being respected. Be clear that if your son does cross the line, you'll get out of the way of the anger and, later, dole out consequences that will relate to his actions.

I know too many parents who take too much badgering from their teenagers. They don't say no or back it up with action. They hang in there with their screaming kid, trying to make things better. Almost always, the parents end up victims, or they escalate the violence. Saying and meaning "No!" doesn't require that you threaten to rip off your son's eyebrows if he curses at you. It requires you to stop playing the game of verbal abuse with him.

Walk away. Get out of the car or the house and leave your child alone for a while. Think of the situation with your child as a tug of war. When you drop the rope, the game is over. It doesn't mean that your child will stop pulling on the rope as hard as he can. It also doesn't mean he's won. It just means he'll be pulling against no one but himself. You're no longer tied to his anger. When you walk away, he'll want to learn a more effective way of dealing with his anger. It's just no fun playing the anger game without someone to yell at.

In your heart, if you know you neither want, deserve nor are able to tolerate your kid's disrespect, your child will get the picture. Be clear that you deserve respect as both a person and parent. It's not okay for anyone in the family to bash you, no matter what his age. You can and should take a strong and compassionate stand as a parent. Allow your child to be responsible for his behavior. If the disrespect does come, don't help him with anything, from fixing dinner to washing clothes to driving him to school, until you're over the hurt of his behavior. Don't punish him. Take care of yourself.

The way out of this cycle is through forgiveness. How do you forgive someone who has treated you badly? For a start, you have to look for and see the humanity in the one who has acted out. Instead of seeing only the behavior, look into the eyes of your child. Focus deeply on how much you love him. If any attitude you have will sway your child's behavior toward you, this is the one that'll do the trick. Your child will learn through your love, and by paying for their deeds through logical consequences. Finally, act compassionately. As the adult, it's your responsibility to forgive first. If you can do it, then your teenager will also ... someday.

Can I Stay Out Until Three?

Families take on the issue of curfew with a wide range of strategies. When should your child be home? To be honest with you, the time you want your child in your house, on the weekends or weekdays, doesn't matter to me. In my private practice, parents always phrase the question in the same way. "It's not *unreasonable* that we want little Kimmy in by midnight on the weekends, is it?" My answer is always no, it's not unreasonable. Then again, it's not unreasonable, in my opinion, that your fifteen-year-old wants to stay out until 2:30 in the morning. Reason isn't the issue. Underneath the veil of curfew, lie the real concerns ... health, safety and communication.

With health, you're either worrying that your precious daughter isn't getting enough sleep, that she's coming down with a cold, or you think that late nights reek of the scary kind of risk-taking. Safety issues include alcohol, sex, non-supervision, as well as wondering who's driving, where your child is and whether she'll be able to stay away from the "bad" people who are out for the witching hour. Communication is a simple matter of feeling better when you know where your child is and what he or she is doing. Over 90 percent of parents relax more when they're in touch with their kiddo.

Let's look at curfew again. When do you want your children back home for their health? Do they have school or other responsibilities that require their time? Does your adolescent operate well on relatively few hours of sleep, or does he need the requisite fourteen hours of shut-eye? What do you need to know (as well as you possibly can) that will convince you your teen will be safe tonight? If your almost-adult can provide you some information, you might feel better about letting him stay out for another hour or two this Friday. Though some teens cruise until the wee hours, most find a place to be by 11 p.m. and stay there. What kind of communication do you need to feel fine about your teenager staying out past nine? Does your daughter have a cell phone so she can call? Can you page her if you're worried? Technology is a cool thing for parents with teenagers. You can get in touch with them, and they can reach you.

I know. Your daughter will suggest that she's safe at her friend's party, even at 3 a.m. Or you'll page your son at midnight and he won't call back. This isn't foolproof. Yet, providing an explanation for the requested re-arrival at home will help you and your teen to understand your boundaries. You won't have to shout, "Because I'm the parent, that's why!" In addition to lowering your blood pressure, a well-thought-out curfew will definitely lessen the number and intensity of arguments.

School Daze

When your child was in elementary school, if you were lucky, you were able to volunteer in the classroom. You knew what your child was studying, because you helped with homework. Two to four times a year, you met with teachers and found out what they thought about your child. Middle school came along. You stopped volunteering in the classroom, but maybe you helped out at the school now and again. More or less, you monitored your children's progress and workload, but it was becoming more complicated and confusing. Report cards and conferences became the major indicator of what was happening in your child's educational life.

Then high school arrived. Where could you volunteer? Where do you get your information? Does anyone even know your child? In my hometown, the two major public high schools have close to 2,000 students each. Each teacher has a student load of about 150 students. And to top it off, your teenage son doesn't want you looking over his shoulder at his schoolwork. He's not a baby, ya know!

Deal with it this way — tell your daughter that school is indeed her business. At the same time, taking care of her is your job. You're committed to doing everything you can to help her keep open as many options as possible. Tell her that, even though the reverberations from her schoolwork will be consequence enough, you aren't willing to completely stop paying attention to school. She should see that your attending school functions and talking with teachers is just one more of the annoying ways that you care about her. Tell her that you're not looking for problems. Your involvement isn't about trusting her. You're just trying to support her. You can't help that you care.

Then, go to every back-to-school night, conference and parent event you can. Volunteer at the school every once in a while to both help out and get a feel for what happens at the high school. E-mail teachers with questions, requests or concerns (because I've found phoning isn't the most effective means of communication anymore). Messages get lost. Teachers have very limited phone time. Now that we're in the 21st Century, just about everybody in the school district is required to be online. Also, turn off your television and read more. That'll help too.

Extracurricular Activities

Ever notice that, since the time your teenager's legs started to lengthen, all he wants to do is sleep. Well, there's a good possibility he'll do more hanging out and sleeping these days and less of the motivated kinds of things he used to do. When this occurs, it doesn't necessarily mean that Junior has developed amotivational syndrome from smoking too much pot. It just means that doing all the things he's supposed to do because you said so, or because it will look good on his college resume, is less of a no-brainer now. Your child may become partially paralyzed, trying to figure out who he is in the world.

I'm no longer surprised when parents come to me with concerns that their teenager is not doing enough, or anything. It makes sense if you think about it. Doing for or with others is harder for an adolescent having an identity crisis. Focusing on yourself is hard enough. Thinking about more than just you, for many teens, is pushing the envelope of possibility. It may take some countenance on your part.

During times of developmental selfishness, I encourage teenagers to do something that takes them out of themselves. Community service, political action, working, sports and school clubs are the soul's milk. They do the mind and body good. And it's always better when a teenager chooses on her own to do something. There is direct inverse correlation between parental prodding and teenager buy-in.

However, if your teenager refuses to get up off the couch, it's okay to push. You can have the expectation that your teen does one thing extra to connect with and give to the world. If she resists, set a time limit. For example, by the year 2014, you want her involved in the community in some way. Give your daughter a few suggestions. She'll resist each and every one. Tell her gently that if she doesn't choose something to do by next Thursday, then the choice will be yours. Be gentle in your insistence. You don't want her to resent the homeless, you want her to learn compassion and caring.

The Sex Talk

"What did the girl say to her date?" "Don't ... Stop ... Please!" This was the first "sex" joke I ever heard. My friends and I thought it so clever that these three words read slowly said *no*, yet when spoken quickly, said *yes*. It was what we wanted to believe girls said to boys. Say *no*, but mean *yes*. Girls who said *yes* were sluts. Girls who said *no* were prudes and teases. Boys who said *no* were "wussies." Boys who said *yes* were studs. We were told to wait until we're married. It was all presented so simply. There was, and still is, such confusion.

Having a helpful and positive Sex Talk is very difficult for many parents to manage. Sex is so intimate it leaves us exposed and frightened. Sexuality uncloaks many layers and feelings. What do I want? How do I ask for what I want? How much of myself do I show? Give? Receive? When and how? Because of the nature of the topic and the culture of our society, few of us have good role models. Most of us learn about sexuality on our own, in dark rooms or in cars, with our eyes clamped shut. Too many of our children have their first sexual experiences under the influence of alcohol or other drugs. Few adults and fewer teenagers have sexual experiences with their eyes and hearts wide open. Too often, we bury our questions, confusions and anxieties. This experience leads to fear as well as uneducated and unhealthy risk taking.

We are too genitally oriented with sex. We still think about the experience as animal lust. Hence, when the hormones start to rage, damn the torpedoes and full speed ahead. The images young people see in music videos and movies, on television and in magazines paint this picture all too clearly. Sex is driven by lust. Sex wears short, tight skirts or shirts opened to reveal rippling abs. It is hot, fast and impulsive. This emphasis on genital satisfaction and the fulfillment of fantasy can lead young people to explore too early or makes sexual assault a fact of life among teenagers. At the same time, I don't believe the answer lies in just saying no.

The alternative is to focus on the intimacy and emotions of sex. I don't want to write off sense-ational sex, but you and I know that the best sex is deeply intimate, within a committed relationship. When you can look into your partner's eyes and see his or her soul, the bells, whistles and fireworks go off. When you can talk and laugh and cry while making love, you're with someone special. And from this perspective (how to make sex meaningful, not good or bad), it's easier to suggest to your teen that sex should be saved for marriage, or that it takes a good amount of time with someone before she should become sexual, or that no one has the right to coerce her to do anything she doesn't want to do. By taking the emphasis off the "either/or" and putting it on the "how and when" allows you to share your values without getting into a power struggle.

Simply forbidding your child to explore what they'll inevitably want is crazy. Teaching your child to embrace the most meaningful experiences within his sexuality and your family values makes a lot more sense. A recent study reported that the two variables that most successfully delayed sex for teenage girls were when (1) girls had a positive relationship with their moms and (2) the moms told their daughters they wanted them to wait before sex. Similar studies with young men show how important a father/son relationship is to a healthy sexual relationship for the child. In other words, talk to your child about sex from a place of comfort and clear values.

Not long ago, a good friend and colleague of mine started to talk about sex at the dinner table with her two teenage sons. They were discussing the right time, how you knew, what you do, and how you decide "how far to go." In the middle of the conversation, her youngest son threw his fork down and said, "I bet no one else's family discusses sex at the dinner table, if ever. If you weren't a therapist, we wouldn't be having this conversation!"

He was mostly right about that. Many parents are nervous about sitting down and having "the talk." Here are a few tips for having an easier time: first, recognize the whole continuum of sexuality that does not include intercourse. Sexuality starts with kissing and moves toward "doing it." In fact, you could say that flirting and handholding are the foreplay of sexuality. Talk with your teenagers about the full range of behaviors. Where do you want your son to stop? What are appropriate ways for your son to express his affection toward his partner? When you talk about your values as they pertain to the range of sexual behaviors (not just intercourse), you won't make sexuality taboo. When you allow your son and daughter to find an appropriate outlet for their feelings, they'll have a better chance of making healthy choices.

Second, instead of having one big talk, have a number of smaller ones. Practice and familiarity will make it easier on everybody. The smaller talks about sexuality allow your child to hear your words. Then, your daughter will stop huffing and puffing in response, and maybe she'll even tell you what she thinks.

Finally, use "teaching moments" when possible. Teaching moments are those times when life holds the door open for you. Say thank you and walk right in. You might be watching television together and the sitcom addresses pre-marital sex. Wait until the commercial, and share what you think. Or perhaps, in the car, her friend will talk about her boyfriend. Join the conversation — tactfully. In this way, the sex talk becomes a part of life rather than a separate, uncomfortable chore of parenting. Good luck!

Of course, you need theory,
but good parenting also requires a lot of practice
and experience if you don't want to drop
the parenting ball.

Chapter 10

Juggling Teenagers

Practice Is Good

I heard a speech a number of years back about how we humans need more than theory in order to educate (from the teacher's perspective) and learn (from the student's point of view). The point was made by teaching the audience how to juggle. I don't know if you can juggle. I can. When I was a teenager, I taught myself the skill for no reason at all, simply by practicing for several weeks. I took time out for sleeping and eating, of course. Okay, so I didn't have much of a life, that's beside the point. What's important to know is that juggling isn't a difficult skill to master. Even though professionals do some remarkable things with numerous flying objects, the basic task of keeping three balls going at the same time is relatively easy.

The theory is clear and simple. Start with one ball in your right hand. Toss it gently from your right hand to your left with an arc that reaches an apex just above your head. Then, start with your left hand and toss the ball to your right. Now, pick up a second ball. With one ball in each hand, start step one. That is, toss the ball gently from your right hand to your left, with an arc that reaches an apex just above your head. As the first ball reaches the top of its arc, start the second ball with a toss crossing underneath the first. Catch the first ball with your left hand and the second one with your right.

We're almost there. Repeat what you just did, but this time start with the first ball in your left hand. Time for the third ball now. With two balls in your right hand and one ball in your left, start the tossing sequence. Toss ball one from right hand to left. When it reaches its apex, toss ball two under it. Catch ball one and when ball two reaches its apogee, toss ball three under it. Catch ball two in your right hand, toss ball one under the zenith of ball three and repeat, over and over and over. You're now juggling.

If all one ever needed was theory, then any of you could put down this book, find something to juggle, and be the hit of your next holiday party. It doesn't work that way. Even if you're one of the three most coordinated parents in Iowa (or wherever else you live), you're going to need a lot of practice, and you'll need to persevere through many failures and small successes before you can take your juggling show on the road.

It turns out that parenting your teenager is the same way. Like the speaker said, theory is not enough. Of course, we need the theory, but we also require a heck of a lot of practice and experience to keep all the balls in the air. And, sometimes they still fall and go boom. It happens with even the most professional and adept jugglers, parents, business people, presidents...

Experience Is the Best Teacher

I've actually taught a number of people to juggle over the years. When I teach someone, I do it through experience. The first lesson is to toss three balls high into the air. Instead of trying to catch them, learners are instructed to let the balls fall to the ground and roll to a stop. I tell my minions to go pick them up. Lesson two is to get very comfortable with lesson one. Dropping balls and bending over to pick them up is going to happen a bunch.

In regard to parenting your teenager, you're in the same situation. Reading this or any other book won't change your life. Theory is not enough. Every day, you're going to need to engage with your sons or daughters lovingly and bravely. There is as good a chance as any that your child will respond to whatever you bring with her own particular brand of adolescent venom. When your teenager does something that upsets you, when she shows you her adolescent anger and resistance, it's the parenting equivalent of balls hitting the ground. This is the second lesson I just mentioned. It's going to happen over and over again. Don't get discouraged. It's not anyone's fault. Don't quit on yourself or your child. Pick up the balls and try again.

I feel like Mr. Miyagi in *The Karate Kid*. "We make agreement. I teach. You learn." I'll give you the theory of how to successfully juggle your adolescent. You keep trying until you get it right, okay? Wax on. Wax off. Paint the Fence. Sand the floor.

Picking Up the Balls

Like I said, with juggling, the first step when learning to juggle is to toss three balls up into the air and to let them fall, pick them up, and then start the process over again. The parenting equivalent is to try to understand your teenager's mindset and developmental work. The longer version of figuring out your teenager requires you to flip back to Chapter 2, *Do I Know You?*, and reread it. The shorter version is this: This isn't personal. What your teenager is doing, though it involves you, is figuring out who in the world she is. Your not-so-sweet teenage child is doing everything she can to create enough space for her psyche to be able to produce a working definition of itself. It's not about you and the job you've done as a parent. I don't care what she yelled at you last night. It's about her and her developmental challenge. It will always be.

Often around the age of thirty, as we begin to see the patterns in our own behavior, we get angry all over again at those who brought us into the world. I see it in my private practice. The old injuries are conjured up one more time. It hurts that our parents did this or that to us. Ideally though, at some point in our adult lives, we begin to forgive our parents. When we're in our forties, with older children and more perspective, our feelings shift once again. We look back at what was, what happened with and/or to us, and we say something very different. "My Dad did the best he could. I wish he could have been there more for me, but it was what he knew to do. His father wasn't there for him. I know that now. And I know he loves me."

Yet we turn around, face our teenager and wonder, "Why can't she just grow up? She knows better than this." You need perspective. Just like your parents a quarter century ago, your teenagers are doing the very best they know how. They're trying very hard to figure out who they are, and the only strategy they can surmise is to push off of whichever parent is nearest.

When I work with teenagers, one of my main goals is to help my clients envision where they want to go. In this way, these teens might start moving toward their own grandest vision of themselves, instead of just resisting what they don't want. It's a smidgen harder for parents to assist their child in the same manner. You might be doing your darnedest to help him see where he's going, and still you get treated like an evil stepmother in a Walt Disney movie. Nevertheless, this understanding of your child will go a long way in helping him be less angry.

Do as I Do

Step Two in juggling your adolescent is to take responsibility for your own issues and decisions with your parenting. A dad I see can be as obstinate as any when it comes to taking responsibility. He does his best to parent while absolving himself of culpability for the decisions he makes. He thinks that if he places responsibility elsewhere, his son won't be angry with him. For example, he didn't want his son to use a rope swing in their neighborhood. Instead of telling his boy "No!" Dad spent all sorts of time trying to come up with creative ways to make other parents responsible for what he wanted. He asked other parents to not let their children on the rope swing. He talked to the owner of the nearest property. He called the city safety officer. He spent way too much time not telling his son what he believed and for what he stood.

On the other hand, the son felt like his dad was being dishonest, and he grew more resentful by the day. It was a bit like calling the Phone Company and trying to get mad. You call with a problem and every person you talk with is quite polite. No one takes responsibility though, because they didn't flip the switch, or promise you service, or whatever. You want to be angry, so you ask for a supervisor. The same thing happens. Everyone is nice and nobody takes responsibility. Eventually, you hang up and scream at your cat.

The son could never get angry directly with his father, because Dad wasn't willing to own what he wanted. The son took his anger out elsewhere. Over time, he became an angry teen who, just like Dad, never took responsibility for his own actions. He became passive-aggressive. Nice try, Pop. With a teenager, it doesn't work to not take responsibility for your feelings and actions.

The point of owning your own stuff with your child is simple. It's what every parent wants from his or her teenager — honesty and responsibility. With teenagers, we teach our children best through our behaviors. Our actions speak louder than a thousand-word lecture. You and I know that teenagers have been known to sneak around and try to get away with a little or a lot. It's important you don't do the same. If you want integrity from your child, act with integrity. If your teen isn't successful in her pursuit of honesty and other family values now, they'll show up later. I can almost guarantee it.

Don't forget, your feelings will come up as you parent your teenager. If you don't take care of your heart and soul, those emotions will get in the way of parenting your child with love. Old feelings that sneak in the back door are generally unresolved and uninvited guests. They're often sad and fearful visitors. If you don't pay attention and own them, you'll parent from fear. You'll make decisions out of your worry for and fear of your not-yet-adult. I promise, your teenager will smell this intention, resent it and act accordingly.

There are a number of reasons the Dad above was unwilling to own his stuff. His own adolescence was a fairly rough one. This man's parents said no to just about everything he requested as a teenager. It didn't matter whether he was asking for money, to see a movie, or to participate in an extracurricular activity at school. The "no" came without any compunction from his mother and father. He felt rejected and mistrusted. He never wanted his own son to feel the same. He managed by never saying no.

As his son entered puberty, there were times when "no" was necessary, but Dad just couldn't bring himself to take responsibility for anything that might duplicate his own experience. Hence, he concocted a manner of parenting that said no, but without taking responsibility for the intention. His son knew this, but couldn't put his finger on what was so disagreeable. It created a lot of problems. Granted, they were different problems from Dad's adolescence, but they were related. Neither Dad nor his son felt trusted. Both were frustrated at their inability to get what they wanted or, at least, negotiate with and be heard by a parent.

Was Blind, But Now You See

This leads us to step three in the guidebook to juggling teenagers. Take the time to think about what kind of person you want your child to become, and parent to that belief. Take a stand and parent according to your values. A bit of a paradox exists here. I realize that I've told you more than once that it's very important to let your teen grow up and figure out for himself who is who and what is what. But it's just as critical that you create some parameters for him to bump up against. Knowing what you believe will help your teenager figure out what he believes.

Think about all the three- and four-year-olds you know. With your mind's eye, draw a composite sketch of the most annoying, bratty, obnoxious kids of that age. You know, the ones that never stop whining, make enormous amounts of noise, throw their food, or cry when the crystal vase they're about to break is taken away. My stomach gets tight just thinking about these little angels.

Now picture the parents. You know of whom I speak. You might include yourself among them. Their parents are the ones who can never say no. They hate the prospect of disappointing their little one and, therefore, give in over and over again. If they ever discipline their child, it's with an explosion of resentment that follows an artificial parenting calm. The toddlers figure out this pattern and become more and more invidious. It's not much fun to spend time with these families.

Want to know what happens to these kids? They grow up with too much control and without solid parameters. It's difficult to develop into the type of person that values himself and others without being given a parental barometer against which to measure oneself. Without a familial pressure gauge, humans become selfish. If we don't teach our children to think of others, they're likely to think only of themselves. Our children learn to think about others through the boundaries and rules we set as parents. The bratty kids you remember are generally raised devoid of limits or carefully coddled through times that challenge self-centeredness.

Now think about teenagers in general. I picture a group of four or five baggy-pants-wearing, baseball-cap-sporting youths walking along the mall oblivious to anyone walking toward them. You'd better get out of the way, because they rarely do. These are the teens that encourage the stereotype of punks. We leap out of their way and think, "Why can't they consider anyone else?" Mark Twain said it well when he opined, "All generalizations are false ... including this one."

Generally speaking, teenagers are selfish. But to reiterate step one of our lesson, they can't help it. Teenagers are, for the most part, thinking of who they are in the world and how they fit on terra firma. It helps them tremendously for you to be clear about what you believe. Then your son can walk alongside your lead, without admitting that you influenced him, or he can choose a different path completely. However, in the process of doing so, he'll have to think about you and the community surrounding him. When you don't stand clearly, he has a greater chance of spending his adolescence walking around in a haze.

This is the equivalent of tossing two balls in the juggling pattern. Figure out what kind of person you want your child to be. When you figure this out, burn this image into your temporal lobe. Whatever you decide to do as a parent, concerning curfew or sex or driving privileges, make the decision based on what you believe will help your child to become the type of person you want him to be.

Don't make parenting decisions because you think they will change your teenager. *This is not the point!* Believe that what you do and say to your teen is your best guess as to what is right. You parenting choices are what you need, regardless of what your teenager wants or does. What your almost-adult does, believe it or not, is beside the point. Concern yourself with your responses to her actions. You see, it doesn't matter what you do. It matters what you do after what you do.

Don't Forget, Remember These Points!

- *Understand the developmental work of adolescence.*
- *Pay more attention to your own actions and beliefs.*
- *Be the person you want your teen to be.*
- *Re-evaluate your parenting choices and adjust them, regularly.*
- *Take good care of yourself.*
- *Keep the faith, as often as you're able.*

One More Time with Feeling

The final step with juggling balls is to start a third ball into the mix. Then watch how you are doing and adjust accordingly. For example, some jugglers learn best by standing a foot or so away from a wall. The wall is both feedback and corrective apparatus for wild throws. It doesn't work for everybody. You may need to work in the middle of a room. Or you may need to go outside so you don't have to battle walls at all. Or you might try bean bags instead of juggling balls. Listen for what you need. Your inner juggler knows to make adjustments, without shame, in order to learn how to juggle.

The corresponding parental maneuver is to make a parenting decision, watch the outcome and adjust your next "toss." Start tossing your parenting decrees in the most creative and interesting ways you can imagine, keeping in mind who you want your child to be. If what you do works, hang on and try it again. If what you do fails miserably (that is, has an unpleasant outcome) then try something else. In this way, consistency is in the message, not in the action. During adolescence, consistency in action can often turn into pattern behavior.

Pattern behaviors are like annoying scratches on your compact discs that cause the music to skip in place. Somehow and for some reason, despite your best intentions, a deep cut has been clawed into family life. When that happens, all rhythm ceases and the same phrase is repeated over and over. If you don't work your way out of the scratch, serious damage occurs.

At worst, you have to get rid of the album. At best, you never find the groove in relationship to that particular groove again. With pattern behavior, stop what you are doing as soon as you recognize it. Identify the uncomfortable repetitions and change your part in the song. Try something else — anything. You'll be amazed at the harmony created by a little shift.

Staying Alive

In every case, take care of yourself. Remain clear about what you believe. Don't lose sight of who your child really is. You'll need to practice often in order to get it right with your teenage child. You'll need to persevere. Keep going, even when things are scary. Love your child like you've never been hurt before. Bend down and pick up what you've dropped over and over again.

My first job in the mental health field was in a co-ed group home with adolescents. Among the male guests in our care were Danny, a fifteen-year-old who had set fire to three houses, Steve, a sixteen-year-old who had spent the previous year in psychiatric lock-up, and Tyler, a hulking teen who smoked too much pot and got into fights with every third person he met. The girls included Sheri, who had dropped acid every day for the past eight months and Darcy, a fourteen-year-old who had become very sexually active at age eleven.

The group home had a very strict behavior modification program that was enforced with as much heart as a staff of eleven could muster. If the kids could meet minimum behavioral expectations, they earned privileges and free time. If they messed up, they went on house arrest. Some residents had a difficult time with the rules. It was why they were living in the home in the first place. They couldn't color between the lines, so to speak. In fact, some of the young adults missed coloring on the paper completely, and just carved their initials into the desk. It took months of holding the line clearly anytime a new teenager arrived at the house.

It was hard for the staff. The kids were tough. Some of them were as good at manipulation as they were at anger. Still, we cared about them deeply. It took teamwork, clarity and perseverance to stick to the system which eventually helped them to find their self-respect and self-discipline.

Regrettably, we weren't always successful. Kids screwed up, took off and did things that felt like gigantic setbacks. At every weekly staff meeting, no matter what had transpired during the previous seven days, we ended the same way. We pulled in tight and whispered, "Just keep 'em alive until they're twenty-one." We had faith that it would change. We had to have faith. You do, too.

I am happy to report that I ran into Sheri and Steve when they were twenty-four or so. Both were married and had started families. They were holding down good jobs and continuing their education. Sheri had finished college and was making more money than I was. Neither hated me the least bit, and we laughed when recalling how good I was at sniffing out their marijuana stashes. Your children will grow up, too. I can't guarantee it'll be perfect, but your kids will mature and become more adult-like. You have to hang in there. Just wait until they're twenty-one.

The Moral of the Story

Last year, my mother sent me a wonderful card that spoke to the hope realized through perseverance. The front was a short vignette of Thomas Edison being asked by a reporter about his 2,000 failures in developing the light bulb. Edison purportedly responded that he did not fail even once. It just happened to be a 2,000-step process to his success. Mr. or Ms. Edison, your teenager is the light bulb. He's a remarkable, almost unimaginable, creation of your labor and love. Your child is in the midst of making a life of his own, extrapolated and synthesized from the values and morals you and every other influence in his life have taught him. Remember, he's only on step 1,179 of his 2,000-step process. He has a way to go before you can see his finished product. But you can picture the bright, shining possibility, can't you? Don't lose that vision. From that vision, excellent parenting occurs.

I must mix my metaphors here. Keep on juggling. Continue to pick up the balls that seem to elude your grasp. Practice, practice, practice. Your daughter's 100-watt, energy-saving light will go on when it's ready. You have to believe the light will shine in order for her to believe. Toss them. Catch them. Then, without question, she'll get precisely where she's supposed to go.

I'll leave you with a joke I thought up while writing this book. How many teenagers does it take to change a light bulb? The answer is "You never understand. Why can't you just let me live my life the way I want? I hate you!" In other words, keep your sense of humor and never take it personally.

Bibliography

Beck, Renee and Metrick, Sydney Barbara. *The Art of Ritual: Creating and Performing Ceremonies for Growth and Change*. Berkeley: Celestial Arts, 1990.

Erikson, Erik. *The Life Cycle Completed*. New York: WW Norton, 1997.

Jackins, Harvey. *The Human Side of Human Beings: The Theory of Re-Evaluation Counseling*. Seattle: Rational Island Publishers, 1965.

Rosemond, John. "Kids and Money (Giving Allowances and Assigning Chores to Children)." *Better Homes and Gardens*. October 1995.

Ventura, Michael. *Letters at 3 AM: Reports on Endarkenment*. Putnam: Spring Publications, 1993.

Cycle of Violence adapted from original concept of Lenore Walker. *The Battered Woman*. New York: Harper & Row, 1979.

Drug Use Continuum adapted from original concept of Michael Connelly. Odyssey Center. www.odysseycenter.com

The American Drug and Alcohol Survey, 2000. Rocky Mountain Behavior Science Institute. www.rmbsi.com

The Karate Kid. Directed by John G. Avildsen. Columbia/Tristar Studios, 1984.

Starman. Directed by John Carpenter. Columbia/Tristar Studios, 1984.

Walkabout. Directed by Nicolas Roeg. Criterion Collection, 1971.

The Zero Effect. Directed by Jake Kasdan. Castle Rock, 1998.

About the Author

John Davis, a licensed clinical social worker, started his professional career as a 6th grade teacher in 1981. His formal schooling includes a degree in education from the University of Colorado, graduate work in experiential education (also at the University of Colorado) and a master's degree in social work from Denver University. He has worked primarily with teenagers and their families since 1983 helping them with all issues teen-related. John collaborated with the Boulder County Health Department to create a high school-based intervention/prevention team and introduced the program into two school districts. He worked in high schools as a therapist for ten years before starting his own private therapy practice in 1997. He is currently certified as an EMDR (Eye Movement Desensitization and Reprocessing) therapist.

For the past 17 years, John has conducted workshops and made motivational speeches for parents, teenagers, teachers, non-profits, businesses and school districts on topics including utilizing humor in your life and work, parent and teen issues, organizational development and team building. He is a trainer for Youth On Board, a Boston-based organization that teaches adults to work with teenagers. John also sat on the National Advisory Board for Project 540, an undertaking that brought 140,000 teenagers from across the country together to create action plans for improving their communities. In addition, John teaches 10th grade Confirmation class at Congregation Har HaShem in Boulder, Colorado. For John, this has been another way to bring spirituality into his conversation with teenagers about the choices they make.

Now that *Don't Take It Personally! A Parent's Guide to Surviving Adolescence* is published, John's current projects include Parenteen Times (an online newsletter for parents) and a book, *Everything I Don't Know*, his memoirs of raising a teenager.

John believes strongly that his clients — all people, for that matter — don't need to be fixed; there is nothing broken. His work is about assisting others to imagine and create their greatest vision of themselves. It is about individuals reaching their highest potential and about families and communities coming together to support one another.